Presented to

_____

By

_____

On the Occasion of

_____

Date

_____

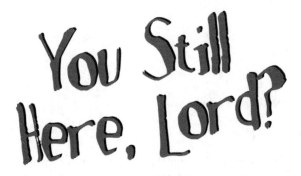

You Still Here, Lord?

The Insecure Woman's Guide to God's Faithfulness

Karon Phillips Goodman

BARBOUR
PUBLISHING

Published by Barbour Publishing, Inc., P.O. Box 719, Uhrichsville, Ohio 44683 www.barbourbooks.com

Our mission is to publish and distribute inspirational products offering exceptional value and biblical encouragement to the masses.

ECPA Member of the
Evangelical Christian
Publishers Association

Printed in the United States of America.
5 4 3 2 1

Dedication

To my readers. . .
your faithfulness has blessed me
more than you'll ever know.
Thank you.

Contents

Introduction

And those who know Your name
will put their trust in You;
for You, LORD,
have not forsaken those who seek You.
PSALM 9:10 NKJV

Living in this world can be scary sometimes. There are problems we have to face, decisions we have to make, and tough times we have to get through. We need help, and sometimes in our darkest hours, we can't see any help anywhere! We easily feel abandoned, alone, and forgotten. We wonder where God went, why He's not here beside us, supporting us in our troubles.

The insecurity you feel is heavy, claustrophobic. You want deliverance and relief, and you want to believe He'll supply it, but your mind wanders. . . .

Yeah, He told you once He would always be here, but now you're not so sure. . . . Maybe He's scooted away; maybe He's busy elsewhere; maybe He's only faithful to His Word when things are easy. Maybe this insecurity you feel is there for a reason—warning you not to put your trust in a God you can't see. Maybe you were wrong and naïve to ever believe Him in the first place.

Maybe He really *has* got better things to do than hold your hand.

Hmm, don't think so.

That insecurity is a common feeling as we face a world where promises are readily broken and truth is subjective. It's easy to become skeptical and to doubt God's goodness and His reasons for being with us when there's nothing we can do if He isn't.

But there's no reason to be insecure about your Father! He's got no time or need for games, for playing with your trust. And He has the perfect and permanent cure for your insecurity: *knowing Him.*

If you know Him, you can never be insecure again. Ever.

Oh, He's still here, all right, as a teacher and a guide, an open book for all your questions. *Know Him.* And never doubt again.

Wherever you are, there He is.

Part 1

To Doubt, to Dare

When I consider your heavens,
the work of your fingers, the moon and the stars,
which you have set in place,
what is man that you are mindful of him,
the son of man that you care for him?

PSALM 8:3–4 NIV

 Chapter 1

When the Insecurity Is Too Much

Where is your Lord? When you picture Him in your mind, is He close and comforting, awaiting your call? Or is He a little out of focus? Do you have to squint to see Him? Do you look around, tentatively, unsure of His presence?

I think we all get hit with these questions sometimes, with our doubts that multiply like junk mail and have just as much value. We *want* to will the doubts away, but they won't be ignored. Then that dreaded feeling of insecurity in our God sneaks into our hearts. Don't you just hate that? I'm guessing that the Lord does, too, because it's such an unnecessary part of our lives. He has a much better use for our thoughts and our time, and it's guaranteed to eliminate the stoutest insecurity in our lives. I think I've discovered what this great endeavor is.

✳ ✳ ✳

"Lord, I'm so tired and anxious all the time. I feel alone, and yet I keep hearing Your promises in my head. But I confess: That isn't enough. I need to *feel* You in my heart, to know that You're still here with me, to rest in Your care," I told Him.

"I need that, too. Why don't you feel Me in your heart?"

"I don't know. . .I'm just wiped out, defeated, unsure of what to do with myself, confused about so many things."

"I can help you with that, if you'll let Me teach you *Who I am*. Do you want to know?"

"More than anything. What do I have to do?"

"Learn. Trust. Stay close to Me when your life is noisy and messy and hard. And buckle up—it'll be a wild ride."

I took a step back and shook my head. That didn't sound right.

"Maybe You misunderstood my original complaint, Lord. The insecurity in my soul is killing me, and You offer me a race course instead of a safety net? Isn't there a less volatile way for me to really know *Who You are,* please?"

"Well, no. But you're already missing the point. This isn't about you; it's about *Me*. Don't worry. Your security is one of My specialties!

Always being here when you need Me is part of My job description. Want to know more of how I'll touch you, heal you, guide you?"

"Of course, but I'm still scared. One bad bump and I may fall back to where we've started."

"You think that challenge worries Me? Wow, you *do* have a lot to learn."

No Turning Back

Well, with that conversation, I knew I had started something I couldn't stop. Here's a little tip for you: Don't ever ask God to teach you something you're not prepared to learn.

I want to know You, I told Him. I thought that was a simple request. Ha. "Knowing God" is not a correspondence course or a self-study. No, ma'am, it's intense, complete. . .the opening of your soul to His.

And as backward as it might seem, we sometimes have to start the journey when we're at our most vulnerable, when our insecurity has pushed us into a corner, when we can't do anything else.

You know when the insecurity is too much, when your life is a challenge you want to abandon. Sometimes it comes slowly, small ripple after ripple of pesky problems that dig quietly away at your trust and comfort. Sometimes it's a crashing wave that knocks everything stable out from under you with one push and you're left shaken, struggling to stand. Sometimes it's both, and pretty soon, you're too afraid to move. That's when we feel our way, with a hand reaching out for God, "for we walk by faith, not by sight" (2 Corinthians 5:7 NKJV).

No Standing Still

We look around to see where God is, and in our own darkness and fear and desperation, we can't find Him. Has He left us? Has He decided we're not worth the trouble? Has He chosen *now* to walk away from His promises to us?

No, of course not, but the power of a debilitating insecurity is that it builds upon itself and overpowers us. We hear the questions and doubts and won't listen for the Lord's responses to them. We're tempted to give up, to give in to the despair, and let something besides the Lord's love win.

If you've ever done that, you know how much it hurts. You know you don't want to make that mistake again. Fortunately, you don't have to. There's an alternative to the despair, and even though it seems almost impossible at first, we learn quickly why it isn't.

When we're most vulnerable, that's when we have to have the most trust. When we can't go on, that's when we have to look ahead. When we think we can do no more, that's when we have to do the most: learning who this gracious God is and that He's *still here,* no matter what. Then the walk we never walk alone isn't so scary after all.

> *Who shall separate us from the love of Christ? Shall trouble or hardship or persecution or famine or nakedness or danger or sword? . . . No, in all these things we are more than conquerors through him who loved us. For I am convinced that neither death nor life, neither angels nor demons, neither the present nor the future, nor any powers, neither height nor depth, nor anything else in all creation, will be able to separate us from the love of God that is in Christ Jesus our Lord.*
>
> ROMANS 8:35, 37–39 NIV

The quest to know God and rest in His love is the path to eliminating our insecurity. And the first thing we learn is that it's a path He knows well. Our lessons start the second we join Him there. He's been there all along.

"Okay, where do we start?" I ask Him.

"I can start anywhere, but first you need to know why you feel so insecure, why you have all these anxious feelings."

"Because it feels easier than trusting, I guess. How can that be?"

"Ah, simple one. Because you feel like you're walking on a dangerous cliff, and you're afraid to trust Me to catch you if you should fall. It's easier to walk fearfully, to hold back, to doubt My ability or interest, but it hurts you. Why do you do that to yourself?"

He was so right about that cliff—I think I've lived on it way too long.

"Good question."

"Let's find the answer."

 **Chapter 2**

Insecurity Is Easy

It can take great courage sometimes to keep trusting God when our world is falling apart, when we fear everything. We can't be trusting and insecure at the same time, though; and in a real crisis, in our real lives, insecurity often wins. We look for instant, tangible answers, forgetting that all answers are within.

How full we are of those answers depends on how well we know God. Sometimes all we know is the messy life we're living. Then it's easy to lose our faith in God's faithfulness to *us*.

How long, O LORD? Will you forget me
  forever?
How long will you hide your face from me?
How long must I wrestle with my thoughts
  and every day have sorrow in my heart?
How long will my enemy triumph over me?

PSALM 13:1–2 NIV

The sorrow that David speaks of is pushy. It's the same sorrow we feel today, and it's strong and oppressive. Giving in to it may seem easier than overriding it. *Let it win,* we say. *Who cares anyway?* We easily allow ourselves to dramatize every doubt we feel when we should be seeking to understand and dismantle them all instead.

The Lord is waiting for us to do that, but we tarry and hesitate, as if committing to that task is too hard for us *and* God. Meanwhile, the Lord's drumming His fingers. . . . *The journey is here, with Me. . . . I'm here.*

Your Choice

To succumb to the fear and insecurity is a choice, and sometimes it's the easy one. To accept the challenges before us and trust what we know and can learn about God to help us deal with them is the other choice.

When we make that choice, we replace the passive fear and insecurity with active interaction with our Lord. It may not seem like the easy choice, but it is the one that leads to discovery and peace, the choice that never stops. Sure, some of our challenges may take years to overcome. *It doesn't matter,* God says, *I'm still here.* And still, we want it all to be as easy as the doubting.

We want to take all of God's wonder and glory and instantly instill it into our hearts. *Poof!* We want to let Him squeeze all our insecurity away and replace it with purified trust, like an intravenous drip. It doesn't work that way, though, because knowing God is a collaborative effort that requires our commitment and dedication. It's a journey within, paved with battles to overcome, yet forever guided by the One who loves us too much to abandon us.

When you decide that you want to fight for the amazing life God's given you, that you want to meet everything this world throws at you with the only Force big enough to handle it—you've already made the greatest choice of all. Living a secure and abundant life will always mean learning *Who God is,* and everything that matters is built on that.

That's what He tells me, even when I doubt.

✳   ✳   ✳

"Why do you look so puzzled?"

"Well, because I'm not sure about this course of study You're talking about. I'm not the greatest student, You know."

"You'd rather keep living in your insecure little world, doubting Me?"

"Well, no, not when You put it that way."

"That's the only way. You always have a choice: a life of your insecurity or a life of My faithfulness."

"After I choose, then what?" (I just need to know that next step, you know?)

"Then one of My favorite things happens. I watch your eyes and your heart open wide in wonder and amazement. I watch you learn to look around to see Me near you, not to see *if* I'm near you."

I love it when He says things like that.

"Sold. Amaze me."

"Okay, let's understand the origin of your insecurity first."

 Chapter 3

Insecurity Is Learned

Insecurity is one of those self-perpetuating emotions because it feeds on itself and gets bigger and bigger the longer it's left unchecked. We learn our insecurity when we meet rejection or abandonment or defeat. And sometimes that can be every day.

You know what it feels like to fall flat on your face—in a relationship, a job, anything. Then the next time you're faced with a challenge in an area in which you've failed, before you can even start to look for a better outcome, you have a little meeting with yourself. You remember what happened last time, and you think maybe you'd better hold tightly to your spot on that treacherous cliff. Maybe a leap of faith is *not* such a great idea after all. . . .

That's fine, in one way. Learning from mistakes is good and prevents more of the same, but holding on only to past embarrassment and disappointment and feelings of loss takes away all your strength and will and ignores God's power.

You begin to *believe* that you're not up to the challenges of your life, because you think you face them *alone*. You learn to accept that sick feeling of insecurity, to stake your claim on the jagged precipice, distant from the Lord.

> *Do not withhold Your tender mercies from me, O LORD; let Your lovingkindness and Your truth continually preserve me. For innumerable evils have surrounded me; my iniquities have overtaken me, so that I am not able to look up; they are more than the hairs of my head; therefore my heart fails me.*
>
> PSALM 40:11–12 NKJV

Teaching Ourselves

Before we give God a chance to live up to His faithfulness, we decide for ourselves a fate that's built on years of doubting our Lord and ourselves; and we are lost, shrouded in a dense emptiness we can't fill. It's a confusion and abandonment we bring upon ourselves, an insecurity we breed and learn. "Therefore the people wander like sheep oppressed for lack of a shepherd" (Zechariah 10:2 NIV).

And what do we teach ourselves in these moments of wandering without God's guidance? We teach ourselves to doubt God's faithfulness. How sad. Our minds tell our hearts: *I've failed or suffered, and that must mean God's not here with me,* and accepting His apparent failure is easy when we've got so many of our own.

Every time we teach that untruth to ourselves, we pull the blinders a little tighter over our hearts. Every time we base a behavior or assumption on that untruth, we unlearn the character of God, and we retreat even farther from the edge of the cliff where He stands. No wonder we're insecure! And wrong, because always "with us is the LORD our God, to help us and to fight our battles" (2 Chronicles 32:8 NKJV).

* * *

"You're only seeing a tiny part of the picture, you know," God says.

"What part?"

"The part that makes you think I've gone away from you—which I cannot do, by the way."

"What are the other parts?"

"All the real and wonderful truths about My love for you, of course! I know when you hurt. I know when you're afraid. I cannot walk away because I cannot be untrue to *Who I am.* When you know Me, you'll know that, too."

"I've learned all the wrong things, haven't I?"

"Anything that makes you doubt *Me* is wrong. Anything that removes your security in *Me* is wrong. But don't worry. I can teach you the truth that will keep you secure forever."

"And what would that be?"

"That I can be nowhere else but here. Walk with Me a while so that you may know *Who I am*. . .and I will remove all doubt."

"I confess, that doubt is pretty strong at times."

"It doesn't matter. I'm stronger. Relax. This'll be fun."

The Lord tells me that and then smiles at the wrinkle in my brow. Yeah, this should be a real picnic, hanging me out there over the edge of that cliff, just to see if I'm paying attention. . . .

 Chapter 4

Unlearning the Doubt

Oh, sure, this little lesson would be fun for *God.* He already knows everything. But what about me? I'm a mess, and now I have to deal head-on with the doubt that is my constant companion. *Unlearning what I'm so accustomed to can't be easy,* I think, *but maybe He's right.* Maybe His love and truth can dispel my doubt—and yours, too.

That awful insecurity we feel grabs us by the throat and just won't let go sometimes. We doubt if God will *really* help us and comfort us when times get tough, if He can understand our fears, or if He knows we're sorry when we make a mistake. "Like a wave of the sea driven and tossed by the wind" (James 1:6 NKJV), we hold nothing secure when we live in doubt, and yet it's hard to shake.

We doubt if we can trust Him to fulfill promises older than the world—today—in our little insignificant lives. We doubt that He would be interested in what we could offer. (Is there anything? We doubt it.) We doubt everything we can think of when we let the insecurity rule our hearts.

It's easy to doubt. It's a habit. It can go.

The Answer

As if our own doubts aren't enough, we have the unbelievers squawking around us all the time, those who jab at us with their doubts and attacks on our faith. We feel hit by all sides, buried under the insecurity of others who would rather doubt than trust. Their arguments even sound plausible and convincing at times, especially when our problems and hurts feel like the world's largest hailstorm with our heads as the target.

We seek peace and protection, safety and sanctuary, and we have to choose where we'll look. No one can make that choice for us.

> I say to God my Rock, "Why have you for-gotten me? Why must I go about mourning, oppressed by the enemy?" My bones suffer mortal agony as my foes taunt me, saying to me all day long, "Where is your God?"
>
> PSALM 42:9–10 NIV

Whether the worries and fears are coming

from others or ourselves, we must replace that habit of terrible doubting with a new one—with learning instead of struggling, with answering instead of agonizing. That choice won't suspend the hail in midair while we run away, but it will surround us with the knowledge of our God— the world's warmest and most comforting port in a storm we could ever hope for.

When we need a new response to the question, "Where is your God?", we can give it from the cocoon of His love. In His faithfulness, the Lord has supplied us with two answers actually, a short one and a long one.

The short answer to any question about the Lord's faithfulness is that He's still right here with you, that you know that, and you feel secure.

The long answer is knowing why you can give the short answer.

And you will seek Me and find Me, when you search for Me with all your heart.

JEREMIAH 29:13 NKJV

✳ ✳ ✳

"Are you following Me here?" the Lord asks.

"I think so, but I need You to explain all this to me, to help me unlearn this troubling doubt."

"Of course. I love this part. But it means some bravery on your part, too."

Really. How'd I know?

"What do I need to do?"

"Be brave enough to trust *My* bravery. Dare Me to be who I say I am."

"And that will take care of my doubt? That will banish my insecurity?"

"It's where we start. And it's the hardest part. Ready?"

Deep breath.

"The hardest part first? Why?"

"Because the choice to know *Who I am* is the most important one. You must do that on your own, but then you'll never have to make another decision alone."

"Okay. How long does this hardest part take?" (I need details.)

"A breath. Take a step off that cliff and look underneath. You can't take the step and doubt at the same time. What's it gonna be?"

I wonder if this is the fun part yet.

 Chapter 5

Stepping Off

Well, learning about the Lord is never boring, is it?! *Step off,* He says. Just like that. Into the unknown I'm supposed to fling myself, casting aside all the fears and problems and difficulties of my life like giant stones. Just sail over the depths alone—oh, wait—He said the *decision* was all I had to do alone. That must mean that if I choose to trust Him, He'll always be here with me forever after, and He'll teach me everything I want to know about Him. I don't know. . . . That's asking a lot. I wonder if I got that part right?

> *"Even to your old age and gray hairs I am he, I am he who will sustain you. I have made you and I will carry you; I will sustain you and I will rescue you."*
>
> ISAIAH 46:4 NIV

Why God Says, "Step Off"

The Lord asks for that decision from us because it's the only way we can learn *Who He is*. He talks to us when we choose to listen. Once we begin that quest, there is no limit to what He can teach us and how far away from the cliff we can go.

He doesn't say that the problems of our lives will melt away, because that's not the goal. The problems are moments in time in which we can step off into God's love and see if He's as real as He promised. The opportunities for that are everywhere in your everyday life, in all of the common little experiences that introduce you to and educate you about your Lord.

Do you think your broken pipes are just broken pipes? Don't be silly. Is the fight with your teenager just a fight with your teenager? Hardly. Every little crisis or encounter you meet each and every day is a chance to claim God's faithfulness for yourself.

If you've taken the first step, the one that says, "Yes, I believe," then you can more easily take the ones that follow, because God's holding your hand in one of His, and in the other, He holds a lesson plan. *What shall you learn about Me today?* He asks.

Every step away from the cliff is a chance to know God better. Every little thing in your life, if you hold God's hand while you examine it, will reveal more of His character, His heart, His wisdom, and His faithfulness. Because no matter how benign or how tragic whatever befalls you, He is still there with you, loving you. That's *Who He is,* and it won't change because we can forever "know and rely on the love God has for us" (1 John 4:16 NIV).

Step Now

Let's take a step today, okay? (He said it would be fun, remember?) Choose something that's troubling you right now. Is it a health problem? A family concern? A job dilemma? Pick one pocket of insecurity and follow this exercise.

Step 1. Hold your problem in one hand and place your other hand in God's hand. You can't do that if He's a mile away, so sit right there beside Him while we do this. Let's use a financial concern for our example, since most of us have been attacked by that insecurity a time or two.

Step 2. Tell the Lord everything that's bothering you about the problem. I know it sounds silly to tell Him what He already knows, but this step is for you—to corral your thoughts, renew your choice, and focus your prayer. Tell Him out loud if you want to.

Step 3. Listen for Him to reveal a truth about Himself that you need to know concerning *this particular kind of problem.* For our example, we need to know the part of God that imparts wisdom and cares about our well-being, the part that is as concerned about our everyday earthly lives as we are. We need to know His devotion to us when a part of our world is out of our control. We need to know that He has a far better plan than we could ever conceive. We need to know that He will instill in us the ability and insight we need to make tough decisions about our lives. Listen. Learn. Believe.

Step 4. Claim the truth God has taught you for your own, *just for you,* right now. Personalize it and repeat it to yourself over and over. Reinforce His teachings in your mind, and you'll feel them in your heart. Yes, He is always the same, for you and for me, but He will reveal to you exactly what *you* need to answer your unique questions. It's an unbelievably kind and brilliant part of *Who He is.* Claim that personal part of Himself that He gives especially to you, and never let it go, because it can never change.

Step 5. Look down. You've stepped off the cliff, and yet you're safer than you were before. Why? Because *God's still holding your hand!* And now you know something new about Him, too, something personal just for you. In one breath, your world changes, and the Lord gets to demonstrate to you His faithfulness that simply will not fail.

Now, you've still got the same financial concern, you say. I know, but that's okay—because when you're secure in God's faithfulness, when you do not doubt Him, you can go and face that problem with a different light. It's not dealing with it by expecting God to make it disappear; it's an approach that says instead, "Hey! God's still here, so together I know we can handle this part of my life." It's stepping out in need and being rewarded with a security only God can give.

And it's only the beginning.

Yet I am poor and needy; come quickly to me, O God. You are my help and my deliverer; O LORD, do not delay.

PSALM 70:5 NIV

 Chapter 6

Daring God

I can hear you from there. How *dare* I tell you to dare God? Isn't that blasphemy or something? Oh, I hope not! Maybe I should explain. . . .

There is never any way, even with all the studying in the world, to know God well enough to know all He's capable of—He's just too powerful, too grand! And He wants powerful and grand things for us, too, and all of it must be built on what we know about Him. Everything we learn and every truth we discover about Him makes us strong and secure, able to go out into this world bold and unafraid, loved and valued.

> *"I will lead the blind by ways they have not known, along unfamiliar paths I will guide them; I will turn the darkness into light before them and make the rough places smooth. These are the things I will do; I will not forsake them."* ISAIAH 42:16 NIV

Every time we dare Him to teach us something new, He will. Every time we dare Him to help us and guide us, He will. And every time we dare Him to live up to His faithfulness, He will.

* * *

"Okay, Lord, so I can dare You to take away my insecurity?"

"Sure."

"And to walk with me through any problem I have?"

"Absolutely."

"You'll never abandon me, no matter what?"

"You got it. That would go against My character."

"Okay, is that all there is to it?"

"Well, there's just one catch."

"Uh-oh. Do I have to step off the cliff again?"

"Sort of."

I knew it. I guess daring God has consequences! The old saying must be true, that we should be careful what we wish for because we just might get it.

Only with daring God to teach you *Who He is,* there's no "might" to it. You will definitely be led into the classroom—where the lessons will begin immediately, beautifully, personally. The Lord loves an opportunity to let us get to know

Him—because He knows that our insecurity is no match for His love.

Your love, O LORD, reaches to the heavens,
your faithfulness to the skies.

PSALM 36:5 NIV

A Safe Dare

When you decide to dare God to teach you about His faithfulness, get ready to learn because He will never turn you down. And if you dare Him to take your problems and show you what you should do, get ready for His instructions that are always clothed in *Who He is.* His integrity frames every command.

When you dare Him to make Himself known to you, you unleash His hand upon your life. You stand open and vulnerable, and your fear and insecurity and exasperation have to face God and see what happens. It's not even close to a fair fight.

Because daring God to be a bigger part of your life is a prayer you can always count on to be answered with an immediate *"yes,"* you will feel His powerful presence in that one breath. He will stay close to you so that you won't be able to think a thought that doesn't concern Him. As He walks with you through your dare, He will delight in your discovery and amazement, your comfort and peace. He knows where you need to go, and if you dare Him to show you, He grabs the chance to be close to you. Why? Because it's *Who He is.*

> *Commit your works to the LORD, and your thoughts will be established.*

PROVERBS 16:3 NKJV

Do you see the cycle? *He does what He does because He is Who He is.* His faithfulness to answer your call is part of *Who He is.* That's why no dare that calls Him close to you is too much for Him. And nothing gets His attention faster.

 Chapter 7

Daring Yourself

Well, apparently there's no time-out in this class. I dare my Lord, and He brings it right back to me.

"Want to tell me about that other step now?"

"You have to dare *yourself,* too. You have to dare yourself to trust Me, to believe in all you learn about Me. Can you do that?"

"If You stay here with me, I think I can."

"Well, why don't you come up with something hard?" He laughs at me. "Of course, I'm here. I dare *you* to stay with Me."

Never gives a girl a break, does He? That blessed choice we make to step off into God's loving and faithful arms is the tiny beginning of a never-ending journey. We often make it more complex than it has to be. The Lord sees it as pretty simple, simply because He is "right and true; he is faithful in all he does" (Psalm 33:4 NIV).

Feeling Secure in the Insecurity

You may feel like every part of your life is a dare—by others, as if the whole world is daring you to just live with the fear and unhappiness of your life, to be content in the depths of your worries or your past. Those selfish dares will only lead you to more hurt and suffering and insecurity if you give in to them.

The dares that get you away from the hurt and suffering and insecurity are the ones that are based on God's faithfulness first and your security second. I know that sounds confusing, but it's really not.

When you frame your dares in God's faithfulness, you put your hand in His, remember? If you dare yourself to overcome a problem, it's because you trust that God will be there to help you with it, *because He promised.* If you trust God to be with you, you know that you are safe in His love and care, and you absolutely *cannot* be insecure when He's holding you close. Understand now?

"You don't have to know everything when you know *Me*," He says.

It's really a beautiful, simple plan.

Not that we are sufficient of ourselves to think of anything as being from ourselves, but our sufficiency is from God.

2 Corinthians 3:5 nkjv

A Predictable Dare

None of us is immune to life's everyday challenges, and while pressure at work or discontent in your family may not be the end of the world, it's enough to cause the anxious, irritable, insecure feelings we know so well. Do you want to dare yourself to overcome that situation, to even learn from it? Then do it, by taking one breath to call on God's faithfulness and abandoning your insecurity to something so much bigger.

When you dare yourself to meet your challenges, you dare God at the same time—and the same pattern emerges: *You dare Him, He dares you; He delivers, you learn.* He may surprise you with the lessons any particular dare will teach, but if you trust Him to never steer you wrong and you commit yourself to listening to what He says, you learn more about *Who He is* every time.

And then here we are again: You learn *Who He is,* how He is faithful in absolutely every situation, and your insecurity is a no-show. It's actually quite an amazing circle, isn't it? And it's one He will never break.

> *Let us hold unswervingly to the hope we profess, for he who promised is faithful.*
>
> HEBREWS 10:23 NIV

Even when you think you've learned all about one of the Lord's wonderful attributes, life has a way of testing that knowledge. He is so much; He is everything, applicable to every circumstance—and yet we often feel compelled to keep checking just to be sure He's still here. The insecurity is pushy, stubborn, just like us. But it can't push Him away.

"If it takes one or a thousand dares to know Me, that's okay. I'm still here," the Lord tells me.

"It's okay to ask You things over and over?"

"It's okay but unnecessary. I will always be the same. It's *you* who needs to change."

"Change how?"

"Change your heart. Don't imprison it in that insecurity you've let it create. Give it to Me and watch the wonders begin. Go ahead—*I dare you.*"

✱ ✱ ✱

God's faithfulness is God's love. He says to me, "I can't love you any more today or tomorrow than I did the moment I thought of you, because that love is more than the whole world, more than you can ever imagine. **That love is Who I am.*"*

To Doubt, To Dare—God's Love

- How have you responded when you felt most vulnerable, in security or in fear?
- Have you ever taken the "easy way out" instead of working to learn about God's faithfulness?
- Are you willing to commit yourself to the quest of getting to know God and unlearning your doubt? Are you ready to start today?
- How have your choices in the past kept you from releasing your doubt? Why?
- How hard is it for you to "step off the cliff" into God's love and believe that He's there to hold you? Why?
- What will you dare God to teach you today?
- How will you let God's faithfulness frame a new dare for yourself today?
- How will you change your heart by giving it to God?

✶ ✶ ✶

Lord, in Your love, *I come to learn how to defeat my doubts and shed my insecurities. Please hold my hand tightly in Yours, catch me as I step off my cliff of fear, and meet me in my dares to demonstrate*

Your faithfulness. Please teach me more every day of **Who You are,** *and wrap me in Your great and unending love. Amen.*

Part 2

To Test, to Hold

Test everything. Hold on to the good.

1 Thessalonians 5:21 NIV

 Chapter 8

Afraid to Test

"Do you know that your insecurity is blocking some wonderful blessings I have for you?" the Lord asks.

"Well, no, how's that?" I want to know this quickly!

"When you are reluctant to trust Me, everything you see is a battle you've already lost, a goal you can't reach."

"How can I change that? I want to trust You, but You know how afraid I am sometimes."

"I know. But the only way to trust Me is to *know* Me, remember? And you get to know Me when you hold Me up to everything in your world, everything that makes you nervous and afraid."

"Then what?"

"Then you will know more about *Who I am*. You will know that I'm bigger and stronger and more powerful than anything. Go ahead—pit

Me against any insecurity you have and see what happens."

"Can You give me a hint?"

"Let's just say that instead of blocking your blessings, you'll be overflowing with them. *Trust Me.*"

*   *   *

Well, who wouldn't want that?! I must have had it all backward! God doesn't *bless* us so that we'll *know* He's faithful—we *trust* in His faithfulness and then *discover* His blessings.

That's a radical concept, isn't it? But it's founded on the most basic idea of all: knowing *Who He is.* And He says that we can do that in part by testing His faithfulness against everything that scares us. (I hope He hasn't made any tight plans. . . . This could take a while with me.)

Perhaps that's even part of what scares us— getting all those fears and doubts out in front of Him. We wonder if He'll notice, and then we're afraid that He'll notice too much. We worry unnecessarily.

> *"Am I a God near at hand," says the* LORD, *"and not a God afar off? Can anyone hide himself in secret places, so I shall not see him?" says the* LORD; *"do I not fill heaven and earth?" says the* LORD.

JEREMIAH 23:23–24 NKJV

His Powerful Grace

Testing our insecurities isn't something we can do alone, hidden away in a private corner somewhere, figuring out how it works as we go along. We might think God would leave us to flounder that way, but guess what? *He can't.*

The same part of Him that wants to give us those blessings right and left is the part of Him that wants to rescue us and be our Companion forevermore. His tender grace is rooted in His unconquerable power—nothing is outside His reach, including our insecurities that grab us and don't want to let go.

"Give them to Me," He says, *"and see what happens."* It's a dare we can't lose.

> *From the fullness of his grace we have all received one blessing after another.*
>
> JOHN 1:16 NIV

Is Testing Okay?

If we're a little cautious about going to God and asking Him to teach us something or explain something, we can let go of that caution right now. The

Lord will never turn us away. He sees every question and every bit of confusion on our part as an opportunity to teach us, to show us *Who He is,* to display His faithfulness. It's not an insult to ask Him anything—it's all interaction with Him, and that can *never* be wrong.

No lack of faith or abundance of fear on our part can ever defeat God's power or ever "nullify God's faithfulness" to us (Romans 3:3 NIV).

We need to learn that testing our insecurities isn't the same as testing God. You may equate "testing God" with deliberately doing something wrong and wondering if He'll mind. That's not a test; it's defiance—and a quick way to more fear and uncertainty.

Testing your *insecurities,* though, is about measuring them against an immeasurable God, about stacking their power against His.

Is your fear overwhelming when it's compared to God's safety? Is your pain unbearable when it's met with God's comfort? Is your confusion oppressive when it's explained by God's wisdom?

The answer is always no. And I can tell you why: because God is confident in His power to come out on top in any test, anywhere, anytime. Nothing can beat Him. That power is part of *Who He is.* We can claim it and hold it for ourselves, too, when we've held our insecurities up to Him and seen them crumble piece by piece.

*"God, who made the world and everything
in it, since He is Lord of heaven and earth,
does not dwell in temples made with hands.
Nor is He worshiped with men's hands, as
though He needed anything, since He gives
to all life, breath, and all things."*

ACTS 17:24–25 NKJV

Testing Unafraid

Everything we have that causes us to feel insecure
can be countered by something in God's character.
When we know what trait it is that we need to call
upon, we don't have to feel insecure. We can be
focused, sure, and confident. And the Lord will be
faithful to *Who He is* every time, making testing
those insecurities not so scary after all.

I bet He knew that all along, don't you?

But how do we learn the right way to test?
How do we learn what to hold on to?

We don't learn by wishing or hurrying or
copying someone else. We learn with the Lord at
our side, of course. How kind of Him to join us
for this new endeavor. And how predictable. He
can work miracles remembered for all time, and
He can quietly and privately touch you in His
miraculous way today. Nothing is beyond His

power, but He knows our limited ability to navigate this journey. He reaches to our level of understanding to guide us through the darkness.

Let the morning bring me word of your unfailing love, for I have put my trust in you. Show me the way I should go, for to you I lift up my soul.

PSALM 143:8 NIV

 Chapter 9

Testing Rule #1

"I'm afraid this will be hard, You know?"

"Nothing's hard for Me."

"What about *me?*" (I'm still the mortal part of this equation; perhaps He forgot.)

"You worry too much."

Well, no sympathy there. Maybe I'll try another approach. . . .

"How will I know if I'm testing the right way?" I ask.

"If you know more about Me after than you did before, if you look around and I'm still here."

"Okay, but I need You to help me."

"Of course. I'll even give you some testing rules. How about that?"

"Wow! You're prepared!"

"Look at that—you're already getting to know Me."

The Lord is so well prepared that He's anticipated our needs! Amazing. But I'm sure that's just part of *Who He is.* I'm glad that one of us is prepared for these tests, because I've certainly felt weak and cowardly at times, outmatched by my strong insecurities. I need a plan, a guideline to help me through these steps in an unknown territory, and a Protector for the journey.

> *He will cover you with his feathers, and*
> *under his wings you will find refuge; his*
> *faithfulness will be your shield and rampart.*
>
> PSALM 91:4 NIV

As I begin to learn my testing rules, every breath comes with an insecurity, every thought is a doubt. But apparently that's okay—because God said that He wasn't scared of my questions. It's my move, time to test everything I know and fear against His power. My choice is made: Give Him all the questions, and look for the answers. What a relief to know He's made up the rules!

Rule #1

Identify what you need to know. One thing about testing insecurities is that it's best to do them one at a time. God is so vast and powerful, of course, that *He* can handle a million things at once, but we're not usually that talented. Fortunately, we don't have to be, simply because He is. How's that for faithful?

And despite our shortcomings, the Lord is patient and ever so tolerant with our stubborn, recurring needs. We can test anything at any time. We don't have to dump everything into one over-loaded buggy and park it on our heart. God will *always* be faithful to meet us where we are.

Knowing and Feeling

Identifying what you need to know isn't as cryptic as it sounds. In fact, it's quite simple and goes deep into your soul. Here's a quick way to put the answer into words: What you need to *know* will always be what you need to *feel*.

You need to know God's faithfulness because you need to feel secure, right? *No problem,* He says. Let's see about that and try to get our limited minds wrapped around an unlimited God—one insecurity at a time.

Is your world a place with no peace, only confusion and disorder? If you've lost your way, you need to *feel* God's control of your life. You need to *know* He's still in charge of the chaos around you.

Or maybe you have to make some serious decisions and you don't know what to do. You need to *feel* God's direction for your life. You need to *know* that He will guide you when you can't see how you can take one more step.

What if you're carrying a hurt so powerful that it has paralyzed you and now stands between you and anything good in your life? You need to *feel* God's compassion for your heart. You need to *know* that He will always love you and help you to love yourself and others again, too.

Those are just a few broad examples, but they show that whatever you want to feel is living in God's unfailing faithfulness—His love, His strength, His care. Anything you need is living in Him. Knowing *Who He is* brings the power of all that right to your heart.

> *Great is our Lord, and mighty in power;*
> *His understanding is infinite.*
>
> PSALM 147:5 NKJV

So what do you need to know? What insecurities are beating on you today? Choose one; then let the Lord show you His beautiful and timely response. That's the next rule.

 Chapter 10

Testing Rule #2

"Are there 'working hours' for my tests, Lord?"

"You have to be kidding."

"Just checking. I never know when an insecurity is going to jump up and grab me."

"*I* do. That's why I'm always here."

Ah, I'm liking this next rule already!

Rule #2

Go to God with your test every day. Once you start a test, you can't stop it, because the Lord won't. He is faithful to respond to every chance you give Him to teach you something new, to remind you *Who He is.*

Meet Him every day with the expectation that you will discover something wonderful and applicable to your need. The Lord will reveal as much information as you can handle—and as much as you ask for. Don't limit your heart to just a little enlightenment.

> *He who sows sparingly will also reap sparingly, and he who sows bountifully will also reap bountifully.*
>
> 2 CORINTHIANS 9:6 NKJV

Make yourself available every moment of every day. Don't miss what the Lord may be trying to show you or the way He'll choose to get through to you with the knowledge you need.

Look at every situation you encounter as a chance to know more about *Who He is*. What you once dismissed as coincidence may actually be a way the Lord has chosen to speak to you. The Lord's power to work within the confines of our lives truly amazes me.

We can look for burning bushes, or we can look for the less dramatic exchanges and opportunities every day brings. I can't begin to guess what chances for learning your life exposes you to, but you can be confident that you will finish each day wiser than when you started it, if you'll only look and listen.

> *"Why do you spend money for what is not bread, and your wages for what does not*

satisfy? Listen carefully to Me, and eat what is good, and let your soul delight itself in abundance. Incline your ear, and come to Me. Hear, and your soul shall live."

ISAIAH 55:2–3 NKJV

A Test of Worry

I worry about my son sometimes. He's so private about everything and tells me next to nothing, just because that's the way he is, and at seventeen I doubt he'll change anytime soon. I've never known what homework or school responsibilities he has because he always handles everything on his own. Other parents tell me I should consider that a blessing, and I *am* proud of his independence in that area and his attention and commitment to his work, but there's a flip side.

The reality of a world where parents don't know their children scares me. I wonder if I'm missing something—if I could be one of those parents who says, "Well, I never knew. . ." when her child stuns her and the world with some act no one could have imagined. To overcome my worry, I've reminded myself regularly of what I *do* know: that my son is an honor student and he is praised by his teachers and church leaders. I (almost!) always know where he is and who he's with, and he's never given me any reason to worry. But living with the barest details of what he's thinking is hard on a mom!

I needed to feel God's watchful hand on both of us. My insecurity about my parenting and a teenager's belief of invincibility were becoming more than I could handle. I needed to know that God was supporting me and guiding my son's life. And it sent me to a test.

I prayed for God to help me see everything I needed to see and know if there was a problem, to trust what He told me, to breathe a breath in complete knowledge that He is still here with us both. I needed to feel His safety, His love, and His assurance.

One day this insecurity was my only thought, heavy and dark. I don't know why, but I do know that I felt desperate and alone when I wrote a prayer to be assured of God's faithfulness in my coffeebook. It was all I could do. (My "coffeebook," by the way, is a diary I keep to record my daily moments with God. The name "journal" seems too broad and "notebook" too academic— but my "coffeebook" is warm and personal where the Lord and I talk.)

The next afternoon, when my son came home from school, he actually *talked* to me for longer than thirty seconds. By accident, I had learned that day of a college that he might be interested in, and my question about that began a conversation I will forever cherish, both for its content and its rarity.

We didn't talk that much about the school but more about some ideas he had about going away to school, leaving home, and what he thought *I* thought about him leaving home. I was able to say some things to him that I needed to say, and he listened. He was honest and straightforward about what he thought, and I listened.

It was a great comfort, and I know that God was sitting right there beside us, next to the dirty clothes on the floor and the twisted video game cables, helping me connect with my son and push the insecurity away. The Lord met me where I was, to show me *Who He is.* In His infinite power, in an unlikely place, He turned a few words into a miracle—no sweat.

> *He tends his flock like a shepherd: He gathers the lambs in his arms and carries them close to his heart; he gently leads those that have young.*

ISAIAH 40:11 NIV

Not all tests come to pass so quickly, but every day will show you something you need to know if your heart is ready to receive it. You just have to look and listen for the lesson.

Through that time with my son, I learned more about God's compassion, His attention to the real or not-so-real fears we face, His ability to work through insignificant circumstances, and His love for a daughter who was worried. I learned to "know the hope to which he has called you. . .and his incomparably great power for us who believe" (Ephesians 1:18–19 NIV).

I'll take those kinds of lessons any day. How about you?

 Chapter 11

Testing Rule #3

"I want to remember everything You teach me, Lord, and build on that. Why do I lose my grip sometimes?"

"Because those insecurities regenerate when you let them. But it's your choice of what you will grab on to."

"You, Lord! I want to hold *You!*" At least this choice is easy.

"Then know and remember *Who I am,* and you can't hold anything else."

Whoops, another rule.

Rule #3

Hold on to what you learn. Everything God teaches you about Himself is followed by yet another wonderful enlightenment about your life and your place in this world. Every discovery requires you to get a little farther from the edge of your cliff. While God's faithfulness will never change, you will change continually when you learn to trust in it. There is no final exam, no dismissal. The Lord has plans for you!

Every moment of growth and closeness to God leads to another. And when you hold on to what you learn today, you're stronger and more prepared for what He'll reveal to you tomorrow. Grab on to Him and don't let go.

And you don't ever have to worry about "jinxing" what you learn or "overusing" His gifts to you. Stretch each character trait of God, and He will just fill it fuller. It's a power nothing can stop.

> *Not that I have already attained, or am already perfected; but I press on, that I may lay hold of that for which Christ Jesus has also laid hold of me.*
>
> PHILIPPIANS 3:12 NKJV

Teachings for All Tests

When the Lord teaches you about His wisdom for your life through one test, and you are blessed with it exactly when you need it, let it build under you a foundation that makes every step a sure one. Let it be part of the base on which you walk confidently and securely in all you do and in all the other tests to come. When you learn to trust His wisdom in one test, you move on to trusting His guidance or His compassion or His vision in another. In God's power, He knows what you need, and in His faithfulness, He supplies it. There's no way He can't, because "it is God who works in you to will and to act according to his good purpose" (Philippians 2:13 NIV).

When you feel God there with you, you'll know your test is complete! Well, that one anyway. Because our lives are unpredictable and frightening, there will always be insecurities to test. But each time you complete a test, you get to know God a little better; and you have some new truth, tucked safely in your heart, to help carry you to the next one.

You can generalize His specific answers and lessons from one test to a thousand others—because whatever your need is, He's already met it. He's already anticipated your struggle and planned a path to reach you.

Many Tests, One Answer

Through these incessant tests, we develop a powerful skill of our own. It's a spiritual one, but it's easy to draw parallels to anything you know how to do.

Remember when you learned to drive? Every time you started that car, you drew on what you had learned the last time out, and you were ready to learn more. Did you ever put on the brakes too hard on a wet road, recover and regain control before you crashed? Or have you learned that there are signs to warn you of a steep curve for a reason?

You remember those lessons well and hold on to that extra bit of knowledge when similar situations arise. Now when you drive, you don't have to think about each experience one by one because they are all a part of you. And because of them, you are more confident in your abilities, and you know what to expect from yourself behind the wheel.

The security in your soul is the same, if you'll forgive the crude analogy. Every time your life spins out of control, God is there. You learn that precious fact through every test you take, and soon the confidence in God's presence becomes a part of who you are, too. Your soul is safe and secure in the knowledge you had to *learn* a little at a time.

As newborn babes, desire the pure milk of the word, that you may grow thereby, if indeed you have tasted that the Lord is gracious.

1 PETER 2:2–3 NKJV

You learn to drive; then you can plan trips and journey for yourself. You learn to hold on to God's faithfulness, and then you can rest in the reassurance that He will be faithful to respond to whatever your life brings. You can be confident in any conditions, in the rain or the sleet or the snow of your days.

You can only have that security if you know *Who He is,* if you've tested everything that hurts you against His power and breathed the results in, deep and pure, like the breath you take when you've been waiting on news—and when it finally comes, it's good.

You can relax. There is no way the Lord can meet you in one situation and refuse you in another. There is no way He can love you through a mistake today and refuse to do it tomorrow. There is no way His power to respond to your tests will ever fail or be inadequate. He's *still here,* faithful and forever yours. The coast is clear.

 Chapter 12

Emergency Testing

"So, how are you coming with the testing rules?" the Lord asks.

"Okay, I guess. I see that You are unafraid of anything!"

"Just another quality you'll get to know well."

"And I'm so thankful, but I have a question. I understand the rules, and I welcome each lesson and the time to explore and enjoy the test; but what about those panic moments, those insecurities that grip me tighter than a morning glory on my tender tomato vine? Are You still here then, too?"

"Before you can breathe your prayer, I know your need. Think of Me as the original 9-1-1 operator. I work well under pressure."

"What about the rules?"

"They still apply. Let's take a look."

So logical and yet so tender.

Rules Revisited

Rule #1: Identify what you need to know. Remember this rule? It's about identifying what you need to *feel* in your heart and preparing for God to meet you there, faithfully, abundantly. You may not be able to articulate it very well, but the same need is there in an emergency.

During those times of stress, we tend to get tunnel vision, absorbed by the urgency of the moment. That's not always a bad thing, if we're focused on the right target. In a time of panic, we need to feel God beside us—that's all. We need to feel His closeness to us so that we don't feel alone. That's because the insecurity we feel isn't as much about the circumstances as it is about our feeling of aloneness in the circumstances. We need God here now, strong and brave. He responds.

> *Through the LORD's mercies we are not consumed, because His compassions fail not. They are new every morning; great is Your faithfulness.*
>
> LAMENTATIONS 3:22–23 NKJV

Alone No More

I remember a long time ago, when my grandmother was very near death in the hospital. There were people everywhere, all focusing on me as her only grandchild, talking to me, staring at me, patting me gently, trying to say the right things. I remember sitting in a plastic chair facing a wall outside the intensive care unit. I felt so alone even with all those well-meaning people hovering over me. I closed my eyes and put my face in my hands, only for a second. My mind and my heart felt as empty as the block walls that confined me.

At that moment, the heavy hospital noise and chatter around me were gone. I realized that I couldn't hear anything except the breath of a God who heard my prayer before I could ask it. In that millionth of a second, the world stopped and the Lord sat beside me so I wouldn't be alone. I needed Him close to me in my emergency, and He couldn't refuse, because that's *Who He is.*

I knew at that moment I had been blessed with the exact strength and love I needed. My insecurity was gone, beaten by my powerful God. I didn't know the future for my grandmother, but I knew Who was going to be with us both, no matter what. That was all I needed to know. The Lord's hand stilled my frightened soul. That was what I needed to feel.

Rule #2: Go to God with your test every day. Looking at every opportunity is part of emergency testing, too—it just happens more quickly. Often in an emergency, what we need are answers and directions, and the Lord supplies them. We need to feel strong and capable, and He meets us with His guidance and wisdom. He's never too busy to respond when you call for Him. If it's an emergency for you, it's an emergency for Him.

Essential Personnel

You know when there's an unusual occurrence, such as a big blizzard or hurricane, and government offices go into emergency mode and ask that only "essential personnel" report? When these emergencies happen, those who respond are focused on the crisis, and "nonessential" activities are sidestepped.

Our emergencies are like that, whether we're dealing with an illness, an injury, a natural disaster, or something else. Every action during an emergency is essential—everything becomes, literally or figuratively, a matter of life or death. We put nonessential matters aside for a while so that all of our energy can go into responding most effectively. That's not a coincidence. And it's a great classroom.

You may find that you react in an emergency better than you expected, that the meltdown you feared was kept at bay with God's hand upon your shoulder. When time is precious in your emergency, look immediately to the crisis before you, and that's where you'll find the Lord, faithful as ever and afraid of nothing, bringing more than enough power to meet your insecurity.

He will be there for the step in front of you, and then He'll be there for the next one. Your emergency is manageable when the Lord is your Manager.

Rule #3: Hold on to what you learn. That story I told you about my grandmother is almost twenty years old. I can remember the chair I sat in, the view out the window of the waiting room, the sound of the buzzer to open the ICU door. . . . I can see myself, alone among all those people, and I can see myself alone no more, joined by God for the duration of my crisis, as if I were the only person who needed Him right then.

I learned about His empathy for my pain, His tenderness with one of His daughters. And when my insecurities grow like kudzu, I can look back to that day when I couldn't even form the words to pray, but He answered anyway. I was blessed to know a gracious truth about my Lord, and I can hold on to that forever.

Regardless of the nature of your emergency, God is the same. Focus on Him, and let Him teach you something you need to know, something profound that will meet you there in the crisis and follow you everywhere thereafter. It's like a calling card that never expires, filled to a limit you can never reach.

 Chapter 13

God's Test

"Test me in this," says the LORD Almighty, "and see if I will not throw open the flood-gates of heaven and pour out so much blessing that you will not have room enough for it."

MALACHI 3:10 NIV

"Do you know what a life of insecurity means for you?" the Lord asks.

"Yeah, I've got a pretty good idea, and I don't like it. It's a life of second-guesses and drowned dreams. It's a life of uncertainty, but there are so many things that I don't know."

"But I know everything. Want to learn something now?"

"Sure!"

"I love nothing more than being here next to you, blessing you more and more. But *you* decide if that happens."

"I thought *You* were supposed to be the powerful One."

He laughs again. "Go ahead and dare Me to prove it to you."

"How?"

"Like everything else, one breath at a time, one choice at a time, one insecurity at a time."

"How do I start?"

"Move over and let Me sit beside you, a little closer. It's about to get crowded with blessings here!"

"What do I do now?"

"You allow yourself to try things My way, and you get ready to trust everything I show you."

"Can I do that?"

"How can you not?"

Taking the Test

Well, that sounded tough—again—and hard to understand. I was confused. But maybe there was more direction in God's words than I first heard. Maybe I was complicating something that was actually pretty simple (just like He said).

The steps weren't that hard to follow: Get closer to God, listen to Him, and accept what He gives. How could that be a "test" for Him? It sounds like a challenge for me! And I wonder if I'm up for it.

It is a big challenge to turn our entire lives over to God when we're so insecure about every little detail. We argue with ourselves about this simple choice, as if the Lord had one.

What if He doesn't really want me to dump all this mess on Him? What if He won't show me how to handle my problems? What if He gets sidetracked and loses sight of my trouble? What if He's not powerful enough to handle my insecurities?

On the other hand, what if He *does* want my problems because of His faithfulness to help me when I need Him? What if He *does* guide me and direct me because of His faithfulness to my life? What if He *does* watch over me every moment and know exactly what I need because of His faithfulness to comfort me without fail? What if He *is* the most powerful Force I'll ever encounter?

Like He said, it's my choice. One breath of reliance on God to meet me in all of these ways is one breath away from the insecurity that oppresses me. One insecurity given away is one blessing received.

For since the beginning of the world men have not heard nor perceived by the ear, nor has the eye seen any God besides You, who acts for the one who waits for Him.

ISAIAH 64:4 NKJV

All His Way

Still, I can hear your protests and your doubts. *How do I put this test into real practice in my scattered and incomplete world?* you wonder. *How can I give a part of this to God to manage when I can't manage even the tiniest parts myself?*

That's the easiest question of all. You don't give *part* of anything to God—you give it all. And you give it to Him by accepting Him into every part of your life. You don't give Him the easy problems and try to fix the hard ones on your own. You don't give Him your good days and keep your bad ones hidden. You don't give Him your thoughts about some subjects and keep other questions to yourself. You don't trust Him today and mistrust Him tomorrow.

Give everything in you to Him, and then there is no insecurity that can touch you. His faithfulness will not allow Him to receive from us without giving back. His faithfulness is reflected in our trust. His faithfulness is the pattern for our own. He's even given us a history lesson to help us learn.

Trusting, Giving, Receiving

In the prophet Malachi's story, the Lord is reminding His people that they have withheld from

Him their offerings. They were insecure, trusting in something besides the living God. "Just give me one-tenth of your harvest," He said, "and your storehouses will be full of crops!" He started at a very basic level with them, asking for a little and offering a show of His faithfulness they could understand—a successful harvest, an equivalent to their salvation in their way of thinking.

Today, our insecurities abound everywhere, from our children to our work to our health to our country's safety—and to the "crops" in our spirits that we want to grow and share with others. We can take God at His word of overflowing blessings, because that which He proclaims rests in His power to permit.

> *"As the rain and the snow come down from heaven, and do not return to it without watering the earth and making it bud and flourish, so that it yields seed for the sower and bread for the eater, so is my word that goes out from my mouth: It will not return to me empty, but will accomplish what I desire and achieve the purpose for which I sent it."*
>
> ISAIAH 55:10–11 NIV

We can give Him everything and watch Him amaze us not tenfold or one hundredfold, but more than our hearts can ever hold, because He said so and He's still here to make it so.

A Sacrifice That Lasts

"For I desire mercy and not sacrifice, and the knowledge of God more than burnt offerings."

HOSEA 6:6 NKJV

Forever wary, we debate how to test this insecurity. It's not so hard, really, because the Lord is always here, waiting, ready to accept us into His heart, as soon as we ask. And what God waits for isn't the fattest calf we can find but the honesty of a sincere heart, the deliverance of a needy spirit.

Everything we do is done with or without communing with God. Every blessing is dependent on making room for it. If we forget the order, the Lord is faithful to remind us. It's an all-or-nothing proposition, and the "knowledge of God" is found only through the sacrifice of our hearts and spirits to the plans of the Lord. And that is a sacrifice that lasts and a sacrifice we can learn.

Learning to Give

Does sacrificing mean to sign your paycheck over to your church? No, that's too limiting and misses the point. Use *everything* God's given you—your resources and talent and mind and spirit—*everything* to know Him and go where He leads you. When you give all, more will be returned to you.

The giving takes many forms, and we have a glorious lifetime to experience them all. The Lord gives us opportunity after opportunity to learn more of *Who He is* by learning how to give and receive. It means taking care of your family, teaching your kids by the way you live your life, or sharing what you've learned with someone just beginning her walk with God. It means making the choices every day that bring you closer to God. It means learning and discovering more about Him and trusting in His faithfulness when He calls you to do more. It means a walk with Him, unafraid and sure. It means, thanks to the Lord, *no more insecurity.*

And when you make these true sacrifices to God, look out! The blessings will overflow like a faucet you left running during vacation. Open the door to your soul, and the Lord will fill it with everything He is. It's a guarantee you can test forever, and it will not change.

*Every good gift and every perfect gift is
from above, and comes down from the
Father of lights, with whom there is no
variation or shadow of turning.*

JAMES 1:17 NKJV

When you get closer to God (let Him in your heart), you can listen to what He says (His ever-present promises and guidance) and accept what He gives (blessings without number). You can take every blessing that He gives in love and hold on to it, claim it as your own, and use it every day. Then get ready for more.

It's not so much a challenge but a fascinating and exciting way to live your life. It's a life based not on insecurities that have no footing but on the faithfulness of the Lord, Who will overflow you with blessings when you make room for them. What a choice.

Wow, that *is* pretty simple. And simply amazing.

Chapter 14

Holding On, Letting Go

"I am the door. If anyone enters by Me, he will be saved, and will go in and out and find pasture. The thief does not come except to steal, and to kill, and to destroy. I have come that they may have life, and that they may have it more abundantly."

JOHN 10:9–10 NKJV

"This is a big test, and your blessings are too good, Lord! But I'm weak (and a little stubborn) sometimes. Living for and giving everything to You gets scary, and You know these relentless insecurities that keep hounding me."

"I know, but I have an answer for all that."

"Well, please share!"

"No need to shout. All you have to do is ask. . . ."

(Did it again, didn't He? Guess I'll file that bit of knowledge away for later. . . .)

"You must hold on and you must let go—at the same time."

"Uh-oh, I feel like I'm teetering on that cliff again when You talk like that."

"No, it's your heart I'm talking about. Hold on to what fills you up, and let go of what drags you down. Hold on to My promises, and let go of anything that makes you doubt them. Hold on to what I give you, and let go of what I give you."

"Whoa, wait a minute there. You lost me on that last one."

"It's so simple."

(He says that all the time; did you notice that?)

"When I give you compassion and comfort, hold on to that knowledge and trust in *Who I am*—then let it flow through you to someone else. When I give you a blessing of riches or talent, hold on to that as proof of My faithfulness to supply all you need. Then give that to others and make room for even more blessings."

"And I can do all this despite my insecurities?"

"You can do all this *because* of your insecurities. If you weren't looking for Me in the first place, we could never embark on your blessed and abundant life. It only gets better, you know, because *I'm still here.*"

How Will I Know?

I don't know about yours, but my world is a little noisy. And messy. And complicated. There's a *lot* to interfere with this journey God's talking about. How will I learn to hold on and let go of the right things, at the right time, in the right way?

I suspect it'll be a trial-and-error process, not because God's not faithful in His direction, but because my life is guaranteed to be noisy and messy and complicated forever. It's way too easy to lose sight of God's plan under the chaos. It's easy to fall back into the habit of believing our insecurities—even if they've been tested and beaten by God's faithfulness—because we sometimes let the pressures of the day overshadow His love and goodness, listening to our own screams for help instead of His whispers of relief.

I'm sure He knows our panicky approach to our lives, and that's why He never leaves us without His absolute and undeniable touch. Getting through the trials and errors, though, can be rough on us everyday ladies, when the challenges before us call for a warrior, a scholar, and a disciple of the strongest cloth. How can we learn to be that disciple, and how many tests will it take before we will count ourselves *forever and abundantly* blessed?

I've made this harder than it has to be, the Lord tells me. And He explains why.

"You're looking for assurances of Me in the exotic and elaborate, in the great expanse of the universe. I can part the sea when it's necessary, but I can meet you right here, right now, in your kitchen, just as easily. And we can discuss and plan anything you want."

"I suppose there are rules for those meetings, too?" (I wanted to be *real* clear on this.)

"Sort of." He laughs at me again. "You want to know *Who I am?* I will tell you, and you will know—if you will *hear* and *understand.*"

"That sounds too simple." (For once.)

"No, just complete."

"Complete?"

"Yes. Remember I told you to give everything you are to Me? That's where you'll find Me and know Me."

There was the not-so-simple-sounding command again.

"You'll be in everything?"

"When you *ask* and *allow* Me, I will be."

I could feel the noise of my life fading like unimportant memories. God had promised to be in my everything, despite the mess and the complications, to meet me in my kitchen, no less, if I would *ask* Him and *allow* Him. Still, again, it was all my choice to make.

He must be serious about staying with me for this education of mine, about rescuing me from my insecurities, I decide. I bet that's just another beautiful part of *Who He is,* the powerful and loyal Lord, through every trial, every error, every question.

Let's find out.

* * *

God's faithfulness is God's power. He says to me, *"I hold the power to meet and defeat every insecurity you have. When you submit everything, you are in trust to My power. Encased in My love, you will know Me, and you will know the abundant blessings I have prepared just for you.* **That power is Who I am."**

To Test, To Hold—God's Power

- How have you been afraid to test your insecurities against God's power in the past? What can you do differently, starting now?
- What insecurity do you need to test the most today? What do you need to know?
- What everyday opportunities to learn more about *Who God is* have you missed or overlooked? How will you be more attentive?

- Remember a time when the Lord revealed something about His faithfulness to you. How have you held on to that knowledge, or failed to?
- Do you believe that God, in His power, has prepared an abundant life for you? What part of your soul and your life are you withholding from Him?
- How will you prepare to receive the blessings the Lord wants to give you?
- How will you trust in God's power to help you "hold on and let go"?

❋ ❋ ❋

Lord, in Your power, I deliver myself, holding nothing back. Please guide me through my tests to overcome these insecurities that threaten to keep me from the abundant life You have designed for me. Please use Your power to reach my soul and teach me **Who You are,** *and hold me close as only You can. Amen.*

Part 3

To Ask, to Allow

"The grass withers, the flower fades,
but the word of our God stands forever."

ISAIAH 40:8 NKJV

 Chapter 15

What Can We Ask?

"I am everywhere," the Lord had told me. *"Go ahead and test My faithfulness,"* He said. Well, if He insists. . .

Learning *Who God is* is not a lecture but a lab, I quickly discover. My part is the eager, unknowing student with a blank notebook and a thousand questions. The Lord's part is everything else. He said so. And He stands waiting for *me* to ask *Him* into the everything of my life.

The Lord is apparently brilliant as well as tolerant beyond measure. He must be a major strategist, too, because it all really made perfect sense: How could I ask Him to be here with me if I had failed to invite Him into my heart in the beginning? Though He can read my struggling mind, He will wait for me to feel the words in my heart. I have to make that choice. And if I ask, can He say no?

God in My Everything

"What if I told You I was afraid to ask so much of You, to bother You with these details I worry over?"

"I'd tell you to review what we've learned so far."

How logical, again.

"I should remember what all the other tests have shown me, right?"

"Absolutely. Bring anything to Me; *ask* Me to handle it; *ask* Me to care; *ask* Me to intervene."

"And You will?"

"Ah, that's the second choice you must make. Will you *allow* Me into your heart?"

I was beginning to get the picture.

"Hmm, I bet that's a great way to know *Who You are.*"

"It's the only way."

"I like it. Will You help me hear You every day, in everything, in even the most mundane things, so that I know I'm not alone?"

"We're already doing that!" He winks at me. "Can't you feel Me and hear Me now? The blessings begin as soon as you ask."

"And You'll stay here, even when I'm a little hard to get along with and when I have a lot of questions?"

"When are you any other way?"

Very funny, Lord. I'm trying to work here.

 Chapter 16

Why We Can Ask

We see the Lord's logic in the way He explains Himself, and yet we sometimes find the most basic point illogical to our mortal reasoning. Why would He tolerate our nagging questions without complaint? Why would He *invite* us to ask over and over things that to Him must surely seem silly? Why would He remain patient and kind and tolerant of our constant tugging on His shirtsleeve, asking, "Wait, what about this?"

The answer is because the Lord can't be any other way. We can ask Him anything, not because it makes sense or because we have a right to know, but because answering the cries of His child is part of *Who He is*. We can ask because He, *the Lord who does not change* (see Malachi 3:6), is always faithful to answer.

"Answering you isn't hard for Me, you know?"

"Then why am I always afraid to ask, and yet compelled to keep checking to see if You're here?"

"Maybe you're not clear on something else about Me."

"Another wonderful trait You'll tell me about?"

"I can tell you, but I want you to feel it more. Understand?"

"Because that's *Who You are*—a *present* God, always as close as my heartbeat."

"Good job! You're learning quickly. Now, I want you to know and feel My guidance for your every second, guidance that will never lead you wrong. That's why you can ask anything without fear. That's part of *Who I am*."

✳ ✳ ✳

The God of all power will take the time to listen to *me*, to show *me* His beautiful plan for my life without restraint, to let *me* feel Him in my soul. How could I have missed that part of Him before?

God's guidance that I crave is something He prepared for me long ago, instilled in me, and wants to help me rediscover; and it's forever unending. His guidance isn't something that can be measured and calculated and divvied out like slices of birthday cake to hungry preschoolers. There's plenty for you and for me. And it lives in us if only we *ask* and *allow* it to. Wow!

> *I will instruct you and teach you in the way you should go; I will counsel you and watch over you.*

> PSALM 32:8 NIV

Close to the Power

God's power to respond to our need for answers is as big as He is. We can ask Him to reach out and squash our insecurities and then guide us wherever we need to go, secure and unafraid. And He will never, ever withhold from us that which is in His power to give.

That's why we can ask. Then the Lord can respond, and we can witness Him up close and personal, matching the part of His faithfulness that fits with the immediate need we have, whatever it is, guiding us step by step.

That's why all insecurities can be relieved and all doubts reconciled—because only God is strong enough and merciful enough to listen to our cries when we're almost too afraid to ask Him. He's also amazingly patient with us as we move closer to the edge of the cliff, as we learn never to doubt that He's still here with us. And when He's with us—which is always—He can show us even more about *Who He is*. The question remains: Will we allow Him into our hearts everyday, everywhere? The choice is ours.

 **Chapter 17**

Allowing God Close

"Hey, Lord, got a minute?"

"All the minutes in the world."

"Of course You do. When I go looking for You, in a panic that You've deserted me and I can't feel You close, where have You gone?"

"Only as far away as you've pushed Me."

"I'd never mean to push You away! How do I do that?"

"You do that every time you let something in your life get between us."

"But my life is full! What do I do with all this stuff?"

"Why won't you let Me join you for it all?"

"Because I don't know how?"

"Because you haven't asked."

* * *

He makes everything seem so *logical* again. He

says that I've not felt Him close to me because I haven't *asked* Him to be here. Guess I really missed the boat on that one. In His unlimited love and power, the Lord must surely know this vacant and uneasy feeling I get when I think I'm left to journey on my own, when the "everything" is heavy and I am unable to carry it alone.

I know that I'm hopelessly and forever ill equipped to deal with this complicated life I live. And I know that I can do nothing if I'm even one inch away from the Lord. I've learned that the hard way and have the failures to prove it. Maybe you have, too. And I've learned that because of God's faithfulness, I can save myself from more of the same when I allow Him close.

Clearly, the Lord has a soft spot for His imperfect children. He knows that we can only become capable and secure in our imperfection when He's close to us, because that's where everything must start. It's not an accident of nature; it's a testament to His design. And that's why He says He'll be with me in everything *if I ask*. It's my plea, His faithfulness.

$$* \quad * \quad *$$

"You'll be everywhere I am—when I'm washing the dishes and when I'm deep in prayer—if I ask?"

"Yes, because I want to keep you close to Me always. I delight in that interaction with you, that time as familiar and unrehearsed as a hug. It's part of *Who I am*."

Who could ask for more than that? I was beginning to understand. The Lord will come close to me whenever I ask Him to because He wants that, too. How can that make me feel anything *but* secure?

✳ ✳ ✳

"Remember, you must *ask* and *allow* Me close. When you let your insecurities come between us, that's when you feel alone in your responsibilities."

"I hate that feeling."

"I know, but your insecurity of being forsaken by Me is strong because you've held on to it for so long. It's wrong but strong. Want me to show you how to always find Me instead of the fear?"

"More than anything."

"I can do it in three simple steps, *if you'll allow it*. These steps are forever available to you; and between one heartbeat and the next you will find Me, *if you'll allow it*. Ready?"

"Past ready!"

Banishing the Forsaken Insecurity

If I want God close to me all the time, I can have that. If I want His heart next to mine, I can have that. If I want His undivided attention, I can have that. And true to *Who He is,* He will guide me on my quest. To say "thanks" seems inadequate, but I'm sure He understands.

God said that these steps would fit any question, any insecurity I might have. He even said they were simple. I wonder what He meant by that? I'll see if I can follow Him, if His steps will guide me where I need to be, if I can trust His plan.

Step 1. Look.

"Look for Me in everything—the light, the darkness, the loud, the quiet. Look for Me in your heart, your soul, and your spirit. Look for Me first in the morning, last at night. Do you understand?"

"I understand that You are my God Who never sleeps—and touches everything that touches me."

"Excellent. Remember this step, and let's move on."

Step 2. Go.

"Now, imagine a time when you are afraid, when you are running as fast as you can from some horror or threat. It doesn't matter if the threat is real or not, only that it terrifies you. Run as fast and as long as you can."

"I don't like this part!"

"Don't be scared. One more step, and your insecurity will be gone."

Step 3. See.

"Still running?"

"I'm about to drop," I confess. Even imagining the insecurities is exhausting.

"Okay, now stop running, and watch your terror getting closer. Remember our first step? Turn and tell Me what you see."

"I see—*You!*"

"That's right. I haven't gone away from you for one second, no matter how fast or how far you run or how threatened you are. Through everything in the world and everything in your mind, I'm here. If you want Me here, if you allow Me into your world, in the crisis and the common, you will never feel alone again."

"I want You here. And You are so true, so loyal to always answer me when I call."

"Guess I can't help it. It's—"

"I know—it's part of *Who You are.* It's all part of Your plan for me."

* * *

Those steps are a bridge to God's hand to hold us close as we step off the cliff of insecurity. We can choose to hope for a favorable wind to let us down gently, or we can *look* with confidence, *go* with courage, and *see* what will not change—God close to us, guiding us, never forsaking us. He came up with some pretty good steps after all.

> *"For You are my lamp, O LORD; the LORD shall enlighten my darkness."*
>
> 2 SAMUEL 22:29 NKJV

 Chapter 18

Allowing God's Word

When we allow God close to us and keep Him there, we can get to know Him in a more intimate way. We can stop checking for His presence and move on to knowing His promises. We can ask Him anything and be sure of a response. We can push the insecurities farther away the closer we get to the Lord—and the closer we allow Him to get to us.

And when He's closer, we can *hear* Him respond when we ask. We can hear His soothing voice of comfort, His commanding voice of direction, His loving voice of mercy. We can hear His words in our souls, in His Spirit leading our own.

I wonder if He knows how many questions I can ask. . . . I'll check.

✳   ✳   ✳

"You may be spending a lot of time talking to me, You know, if You answer everything I ask. Is that a problem?"

"Nothing's a problem."

"What if You don't have the answers?"

"That sounds like an insecurity to Me. . . ."

"Oops, guess it does, sorry. You wouldn't happen to have an answer for it, would You?"

"For that and everything else you could ever imagine."

"How's that?"

"Because whatever you need to ask, I've already answered."

"How?"

"Because—say it with Me—it's part of *Who I am.* Having the answers for your questions before you can even ask them is part of My faithfulness to you."

"Always?"

"My time is your time."

"Can I have some of it now?"

"What do you think?"

There He goes again.

Praise be to God, who has not rejected my prayer or withheld his love from me!

PSALM 66:20 NIV

Questions of What

Okay, the Lord says that He has all my answers

already. He's prepared them for me before I need them. I don't have to wonder. He's taken care of all my insecurities before I even know I have them! Well, that's a welcome relief. But sometimes it takes us a long time to believe and accept it, doesn't it?

We go to Him with questions about everything that touches us, and we wonder: How could He have answered everything already? How could He possibly know every mess we were going to make even before we were born? Those nagging questions batter us for years, and yet He's not worried. I guess anxiety and a lack of confidence aren't a part of *Who He is.*

Still, we always have a lot of *what* questions. We wonder what to do in every situation. We wonder what our roles on this earth are. We wonder what the future holds. We wonder what the rules must be for surviving this frightening and hard-to-understand world.

And God has an answer that guides us in every concern. His Son spoke a few simple words to answer every *what* question we can have—the basis for everything we'll ever do. The Lord simplified for us and the suspicious Pharisees the very complex way we have at looking at things.

Jesus replied: " 'Love the Lord your God with all your heart and with all your soul

*and with all your mind.' This is the first
and greatest commandment. And the second
is like it: 'Love your neighbor as yourself.' "*

MATTHEW 22:37–39 NIV

Every *what* question we have can be answered
with Jesus' answer. If we use our love for God and
our love for others as a signpost, then we will
never go the wrong way. If we've gotten ourselves
into trouble, the only way out is through our love
for God and our love for others. If we're doubtful
or afraid, defeated or deflated, our love for God
and our love for others brings the security we
need to our hearts, because it's the security of
Jesus' "bottom line," the essential that makes
everything else unimportant.

When we love God and love others, we are in
touch with God's guidance, because then we always
know what to do next. Every action based on these
commands will be right. We are living a part of His
faithfulness that is practical and tangible when we
live out our love for God and our love for others. We
will find that every answer to every question is a part
of Jesus' answer. How much simpler could it be?

If the Lord boiled everything He wanted us to
know down to these two thoughts, don't you think
they must be enough to guide us securely where
we need to go? Don't you think everything you do
that meets these commands must be in His will?

Don't you think that in His faithfulness, God will guide you to the places in your life where you can do these two essential things best?

Every *what* question is answered by either loving God or loving others. And that's never hard to understand.

> *Now by this we know that we know Him,*
> *if we keep His commandments.*

> 1 JOHN 2:3 NKJV

Questions of How

After we get the *whats* answered, forever pushy as we are, we want to know *how*. We want to know how we'll be able to put into practice the answers to our questions, how to respond, how to hear, how to love. We lack confidence in ourselves with the *hows* quite a bit, and we need constant reinforcement from our Lord.

We wonder how, in our insecure little huddles in which we cower, we can ever do the work He calls us to do. How will we—if we did happen to hear God's instructions correctly—ever find the energy, the ability, and the power to meet those tasks? How will we *know* if we're following God's guidance?

We will know if we allow God in the middle of our work, because He will make sure that we understand and follow Him correctly because it's part of *Who He is.* Our stubbornness or inattentiveness or hesitancy is no match for Him. He is the Master, the Designer, and the Guide. And He is too faithful to His plans to ever walk away from them. Grant Him entry into your questions, and you'll find your answers. You'll be amazed at how you're able to respond to what He puts before you.

What once may have seemed too much to bear—maybe leading a group of people just like you in a Bible study—is doable because you're not alone. Or maybe even reaching out to someone you don't know, in compassion and friendship, is scary to you. You'll find that you can do that if the Lord has led you there because He's with you, because "He who has begun a good work in you will complete it until the day of Jesus Christ" (Philippians 1:6 NKJV).

Whatever is *directed* by the Lord will be *completed* by the Lord, in the way He has chosen. You can go back and test each step if you need to, measure each fussy insecurity against Him time and again if you want. You can do whatever you need to do to learn more about God so that all of your questions have answers, even though they are all wrapped up in Jesus' answer. Every day you will discover the traits in the Lord that will guide you through all the *hows* of your life.

✳ ✳ ✳

"Your insecurity has no foundation here, don't you see?"

"But I feel a little small in all of these ideas and tasks and jobs."

"Don't you know—I will give you the exact task to meet your exact strengths and abilities, those you have now or those you will build. My judgment is infallible."

"And if I can count on that, my insecurity is invisible. I like knowing this!"

"Good, there's more. . . ."

Questions of Why

For our light and momentary troubles are achieving for us an eternal glory that far outweighs them all.

2 CORINTHIANS 4:17 NIV

While we're sometimes able to grasp the *what* and the *how* of our lives, we are often stumped with the *why.* Scared and confused, we build a bunker of insecurity and try desperately to hide from and forsake God. We deny His faithfulness because we can't find our own.

We ask *why* a lot when times are tough. *Why are You doing this to me, Lord?* we scream, because we can't do anything else. We can't understand what's happening, and we can't see how to respond, so we throw our hands up in irritation and exasperation and lay all our insecurities out for God to see. *How can He call these troubles* "light and momentary?" we want to know. *Explain* that, we challenge.

And, honest and responsive as always, He does. Our troubles aren't the problem—it's any lack of knowledge about *where God is* in the troubles that hurts us.

A strong security in the Lord's perfect vision, in His clarity that never fails, is what comforts us when we ask *why.* When we believe He's standing a breath away, we can look past the troubles to something wonderful yet to come because He promised blessings without end. And we can recover and carry on.

If that sounds too trite and convenient for you, remember that you are not an idle passenger in your life. The troubles that cause you to check for God's presence are the ones that will teach you more about *Who He is:* the One who sees all and prepares for all, the One who stands ready to calm your troubled heart and give meaning to your insecure spirit.

The Other Question

If we will allow ourselves to step back a moment and look at what's happening, we'll see that we're quite possibly failing to ask *ourselves* the question that needs answering. There is still something to learn when we have to ask, *Why am I questioning if God is here with me?*

Perhaps allowing us to ask that question is the Lord's way of teaching us about Himself, of getting us to move a little closer to the edge of the cliff, with a little more trust in our hearts. When that trust gets strong enough, questioning if God is still with us is something we'll never do. The *why,* which often seemed like the most perplexing question, becomes the least significant when we know God's faithfulness to His plan.

Maybe you think it's only a conditioned reflex to tell yourself to "trust God" during times of struggle, but it's a profound step when you truly do that. Really, honestly, completely trusting God isn't about wishing your troubles away. It's about knowing Who's in charge whether the troubles go or stay. It's about carrying on with a faith in a God who holds everything, starting with you, deep in His heart. It's a security He gives when you ask for it.

The *why* questions give way to the *what* and the *how* (where all the action is) when we allow the Lord to walk us through the dark hours. Being the Light to guide us through the scary night, no matter how long it lasts, is another one of His attributes, one He loves to demonstrate. In His faithfulness day by day, God's answers to your insecurities arrive when you allow Him to intervene in your darkness. Now's a good time, don't you think?

Chapter 19

Allowing God's Intervention

No discipline seems pleasant at the time, but painful. Later on, however, it produces a harvest of righteousness and peace for those who have been trained by it.

HEBREWS 12:11 NIV

"Stay, Lord! Work Your magic!" I tell Him.

"There's no magic, only change. Is that what you want?"

"I don't know; is it?"

He laughs at my lack of conviction, and He knows my troubled spirit.

"You don't have to ever fear the changes and challenges of your life. The change I want to work in you is always the same, from lost to found, from alone to accompanied, from insecure to secure. It's all about the change in your position—from there to here, close to Me."

"You're telling me that during these tough times, You're always the same. It's me who must allow a change in myself?"

"And I'll help you, if you'll let Me."

"Permission granted! Change me, grow me, move me now."

Learning Not to Fear

We're not always ready to embrace change or even to accept it into our everyday lives. We think we're not prepared or don't have enough time. We fear the unknown, and we resist what we think of as punishment for a life poorly led. The Lord sees us differently, and there is no reason to fear any change that is orchestrated by Him. He who never changes stands ready for *us* to change so that we can be more like Him. That is the discipline of learning *Who He is,* so that we will learn who we can become.

Allowing the Lord's intervention into our lives means trusting Him to honor the part of Himself that watches every step we take. His conscientiousness, His attention, His obsession with leading us—it's all part of His faithfulness.

"For I know the plans I have for you,"
declares the LORD, "plans to prosper you

and not to harm you, plans to give you
hope and a future. Then you will call upon
me and come and pray to me, and I will
listen to you. You will seek me and find me
when you seek me with all your heart."

JEREMIAH 29:11–13 NIV

God's discipline and intervention are not an end but the means. It's the way we learn to trust His motives and uncompromising loyalty, the move we make to allow Him into our darkness. We can take His hand and allow the changes in ourselves that move us closer to the light of His guidance.

God is light; in him there is no darkness at
all. If we claim to have fellowship with
him yet walk in the darkness, we lie and do
not live by the truth. . . . Whoever loves his
brother lives in the light, and there is noth-
ing in him to make him stumble.

1 JOHN 1:5–6; 2:10 NIV

There is nothing to fear about the kind of changes that God wants. There is nothing to fear in your past or your future when you give both to Him. There is nothing to fear in His discipline because it's given in His love, steeped in His power, and displayed in His guidance.

Everything He teaches you matches exactly what you need. It's that simple. If you didn't need to grow and learn and evolve, He'd put you in a corner in the dark and leave you there. But that's not what He does. He leads you out into the light, walks beside you, and points out one truth after another that you've failed to learn so far.

Maybe you need discipline and teaching in the area of a bad temper, for example. Do you think that God will remove you from all situations that could provoke your temper so that you don't have to deal with that little splash of darkness? Probably not. Instead, you'll find yourself time and again confronting your weakness and having to make a choice about how you'll respond. If you ask the Lord to show you how to deal with it and allow Him to guide you, you'll experience His faithfulness through His discipline. It's not hard; it's a choice.

With that example or a million others, you can use this four-step process to grow, move, and change—to become more like Jesus, to walk in the light, to experience the security of the Lord's guidance every single day. We can change because He doesn't.

Jesus Christ is the same yesterday and today and forever.

HEBREWS 13:8 NIV

Guiding Our Moves

Step 1. The Questioning.

What kind of intervention do you need in your life? Do you want God to find you, to redeem you, to comfort you, to direct you? Whatever you need Him to bring into your life, He can abundantly supply, but you have to know what you're seeking before you can allow it. That's not a limit on the Lord's power but a need for focus from your heart. And it's not as complicated as it sounds.

A simple prayer of "Lord, please help me see what I'm missing" will cause Him to tap you on the shoulder and say, *"Hey, here I am."* And whatever you need in your life to change your blindness to discovery, He will make available to you.

Asking is the beginning. And in His answers, you will become intimately in touch with the part of *Who He is* that meets your need. There's nothing to fear when only something better will result from the asking, and that's guaranteed.

Step 2. The Shedding.

When we're ready to accept the Lord's intervention, we have to make room for it. That means getting rid of whatever is in our way, whatever is standing between us and God. Maybe it's a stubborn attachment to your own way of doing something. Maybe it's a grudge you won't forgive. Maybe it's a doubt that God is willing to bother with your troubles.

You can feel when something is in the way when you try to talk to God. You know when He's standing at the door of your heart, but you're a foot away, holding whatever you're trusting more than you're trusting Him. You can't allow His intervention into your life until you clear the path for it. And, if you need help doing that, too, guess Who's there to give it to you?

> *If I had cherished sin in my heart, the Lord would not have listened; but God has surely listened and heard my voice in prayer.*
>
> PSALM 66:18–19 NIV

Like a dusty cellar during spring-cleaning, open yourself to the Lord's touch. Let Him see all the mess you've made so He can help you get rid of it. Talk to Him—daily, continually, as you live every moment of your life. Listen for the subtle ways He'll let you know when something's in the way.

It's that unsettling feeling that nags on your mind; it's that sorrow in your heart that won't let you move on to better things. Sometimes, the Lord will bring you back over and over again to the same annoyance until you finally look at it and deal with it. If you acknowledge it and listen to what the Lord is saying, you can move it out of the way. You can "get rid of all bitterness, rage and anger, brawling and slander, along with every form of malice" (Ephesians 4:31 NIV).

If you don't listen for God's guidance, those little things that you're allowing to block the changes God has chosen for you will grow until you can't see around them. They'll take up the space God has designed for your wonder and amazement—until you choose to kick them out of your way. Do that, and you've made room for something far better. When you can see clearly, you're ready for your next move.

Step 3. The Choosing.

The Lord is forever faithful to His decision to give us free will. It's always our choice what we allow into our lives. When we choose to allow a change in our hearts, we're ready to allow His intervention even further. When we've chosen a better path for ourselves than the one we've been walking, we're letting *Him* direct the walk. When we've chosen light instead of darkness, the discoveries dawn.

This part of your move won't always reveal some immediate change that the rest of the world sees. It doesn't matter. The change is all about what happens inside your heart and soul, about what happens between you and your Lord.

Choosing to follow God brings security to your spirit. Your choice allows you to walk a path that is safer and more secure because it's paved with your trust and confidence in a God you are beginning to know well. It's walking every step on that path with the absolute assurance that the Lord is there, too, right beside you. It's a discipline that you not only allow but welcome, because there's nothing scary about it.

Making this choice is stepping off the cliff with your eyes closed, reaching for the hand and the heart of the One you know will be there to catch your own.

Step 4. The Continuing.

Allowing God's intervention into our lives is a *habit*. It's a choice that we make over and over again, knowing that He's there to answer every question we ask, allowing us to go through these steps as often as we need. When we know that and because *we know Him,* every action, word, movement, and choice is a change from insecure to secure.

Through the constant measuring of our choices against God's direction, we can allow Him to intervene in every aspect of our lives—from the smallest to the largest—because our Lord is a creature of habit, too. He will never fail to intervene when we allow it. And He'll surprise and amaze us with the blessings He pours out on us when we look to see Him close to us.

✳ ✳ ✳

"So, what's it gonna be?" the Lord asks. "Will you make a choice for change and allow My intervention?"

"Daily! I want the security that comes only from You."

"It's always here in so many ways, even when your challenges keep coming."

"That sounds like I'm about to learn something else about You."

"You *are* paying attention!"

 Chapter 20

Giving Thanks, Asking for More

Give thanks in all circumstances, for this is God's will for you in Christ Jesus.

1 THESSALONIANS 5:18 NIV

The challenges and tests in our lives never seem to subside, do they? And if we ever think we've escaped a few storms, another one comes around to blindside us at the most delicate moment. What do we do then? Where is our Lord? The insecurity is all we can see, and we need escape. But that's not what we hear God telling us. That's not what we find when we look for Him.

He offers a seemingly contradictory command: *Give thanks for everything.* And we are left with a gift that we often misunderstand, a gift that is a reward—not a platitude, a sign of His faithfulness—not His abandonment.

Thanking in Advance

As we give thanks for everything, we need to remember that it is a gratitude in *advance* of blessings *yet to come,* not a thankfulness for something we can't understand.

We have a hard time trying to be genuinely "thankful" for a problem in our lives, for an injustice or a hurt. The Lord knows that's tough for us because He knows *us.* That's why this command that appears senseless is actually so simple, why it's all about *asking* and *allowing* Him into our lives.

> *This is the confidence we have in approaching God: that if we ask anything according to his will, he hears us. And if we know that he hears us—whatever we ask—we know that we have what we asked of him.*

1 JOHN 5:14–15 NIV

When we "give thanks in all circumstances," we are giving thanks for *God's faithfulness* in all circumstances, for how He'll inspire the creativity and ingenuity He gave us, for how we'll grow in this experience and all others to come. See? We're not faking a gratitude for something that makes no sense, but we're living a thankfulness for the Lord's faithfulness to rescue us from our insecurity in the present and the future.

It's a matter of knowing *Who He is,* of trusting Him to meet us in the mess and show us His will for our lives. Being grateful for the Lord's intervention in and attention to our lives doesn't make the troublesome circumstances disappear, but it brings Him closer to the edge of the cliff, so that our steps are sure, our way lighted. And we build on every inch.

Asking Again

I know that it can be terrifying to surrender to the Lord's will in a situation in which you feel forsaken and rejected. But that's the time when it's most important and effective! As long as we are reluctant to embrace the circumstance that terrifies us, we'll never see all of the blessings the Lord has hidden there. As long as we hold Him at arm's length, we can't move through and past the pain to get to the promise.

And we can trust His promise to supply everything we need to deal with what's happening to us, because the Lord will not waste any opportunity in our lives. He will teach you in the situation you face today so that you will be better equipped to handle the one that comes tomorrow. His faithfulness is full and complete, and our knowledge of *Who He is* grows as long as we allow it.

> So then, just as you received Christ Jesus as Lord, continue to live in him, rooted and built up in him, strengthened in the faith as you were taught, and overflowing with thankfulness.

COLOSSIANS 2:6–7 NIV

Creating Your Own Cause

Do you know that you don't have to wait for a difficult circumstance to benefit from this part of the Lord's faithfulness? You can get to know God more by going to Him with every idea you have, every opportunity, and every choice.

What do you feel compelled to do with your life? Are you afraid, nervous, or insecure about it? Thank God for the ways in which He will guide you to the decisions you need to make. Then take hold of the tools He's given you to accomplish your goals. No one ever said life was easy, but you can give thanks that your life is *directed* by a God who will not steer you wrong.

Test this promise today. *Trust* in God's control of everything. *Thank* Him for the life you're living, and *ask* Him what lessons and blessings await. *Allow* Him to guide you through His plan, and *know* that you will never walk the jagged edge of your cliff alone.

> *Unto the upright there arises light in the darkness. . . . He will not be afraid of evil tidings; his heart is steadfast, trusting in the LORD.*
>
> PSALM 112:4, 7 NKJV

✱ ✱ ✱

"You may have to remind me of this part of Your plan now and then," I tell Him.

"Okay, but it's easy to remember if you keep your focus on Me, instead of the circumstance."

"That will take care of my insecurity?"

"That will take care of everything. When you look at Me, your eyes are open to all that I can give you and show you. When you look elsewhere, you look alone."

"I don't want to be alone!"

"Neither do I. Join Me, won't you? I'm right here, at the cliff's edge."

"Okay, I get it. Thank You for catching me—every time."

 Chapter 21

Accepting His Faithfulness

The more we ask and allow God into our lives, the more we realize that He wasn't kidding—it's a wild ride! There is always something new, always some beautiful surprise or rewarding challenge we could have never imagined. Our habit of asking God what He wants us to do with these opportunities brings us face-to-face with Him, in direct contact with evidence of His faithfulness. We learn to rely on that *first*, to consult Him *first*, and then to prepare for our move even closer to Him. It becomes a blessed way to live.

* * *

"Do you see what is yours for the asking, what I so want to give you?"

"I'm getting there! It's almost hard to believe

that You have prepared so much for *me*, that You're *always* still here."

"Don't make it hard. Accept My love, and use it to answer every insecurity you'll ever have. You can do that because My love won't change, remember?"

"Because it's part of *Who You are.*"

"Yes, and because it's part of who *you* are."

Now that's a security to hold on to!

Your eyes saw my unformed body. All the days ordained for me were written in your book before one of them came to be.

PSALM 139:16 NIV

Because the Lord is forever faithful, we can ask Him anything. Yet we find more and more that the questions change. They mature as we do. The more we allow God close, the more He reveals to us. The more we accept His judgment and wisdom and vision, the more He trusts us to use our knowledge well. The more we submit to His power, the more blessed we are.

He Meets Us Where We Are

One of the Lord's traits we learn about is His

ability to be everywhere and everything we need, at the exact moment we need Him. He never puts us on hold or tells us to take a number. We hear Him speak when we listen.

God meets us in the way that we can understand. When we are beginning to explore a relationship with Him, He seems basic and quiet. As we grow and accept more of the changes He wants to bring to our lives, He becomes more complex and massive to us. He shows us what allowing Him into our lives is all about.

As we adopt the Lord's faithfulness into our hearts and He reveals more through every step we take, we see that it's not only a wonderful truth to hold on to. It's also a delightful responsibility to grow into, because "from everyone who has been given much, much will be demanded; and from the one who has been entrusted with much, much more will be asked" (Luke 12:48 NIV).

Asking and *allowing* God into our lives becomes living our lives as God *asks* and *allows* us to. His Spirit guides us through our flesh-and-blood encounters. And the more we know about our Lord, the more we know about our world. We can fight any battle and weather any storm because He's right here, always beside us, always answering whatever we ask with the answer He prepared before we even knew the question! His answer is in the peace of His Son, which is as dependable as His faithfulness.

"Peace I leave with you, My peace I give to you; not as the world gives do I give to you. Let not your heart be troubled, neither let it be afraid."

JOHN 14:27 NKJV

✳ ✳ ✳

"Okay, Lord, let's fling open the doors and get me out into the light!"

"There is much to explore, many changes to make, lots to learn and do," He says.

"I have dozens of questions already. And You have all the answers, right?"

"Of course. Will you trust My guidance?"

"I will! I want to hear Your voice and follow Your commands."

"That's not hard, if You believe."

"And that's not hard, if You're still here."

✳ ✳ ✳

We don't have to be afraid or doubtful or lost or anything else that questions the Lord's guidance and control over our lives. We can *ask* Him to be here, *allow* Him to be here, and together march through the most daunting darkness with a peace that calms our hearts and a truth that never changes.

And then, faithful to *Who He is,* the Lord provides us a place of rest for our weary spirits, a retreat unto Him where we can renew and relish everything we've learned. He is forever faithful to be our safe and lighted sanctuary.

> *"I have come as a light into the world, that whoever believes in Me should not abide in darkness."*
>
> JOHN 12:46 NKJV

* * *

God's faithfulness is God's guidance. *He says to me, "Through My guidance, I will lead you where you need to go; I will teach you what you need to learn; I will bring security to your heart and soul. When you ask and allow Me into your life, you will learn that I am the God Who guides you by walking with you, through the darkness, into the light.* ***That guidance is Who I am."***

To Ask, To Allow—God's Guidance

- What kinds of questions have you been afraid to ask the Lord? Why?
- How have you failed to allow God close to you in the past? Can you follow His steps to banish your feelings of insecurity?
- How will you find security in your life

by following the two great commands Jesus has given us? What will you do today that reflects your obedience to those commands?

- How have you failed to trust God to be with you through your tough times? How did it feel to put your trust elsewhere?

- Why have you been afraid to allow God's intervention in your life? What is in the darkness that you don't want Him to see? How can you make a better habit for yourself, starting today?

- What seemingly unfortunate circumstance will you give thanks for today? How will you listen for God's revelations about how He'll prepare you to respond to your crisis?

- Accepting God's faithfulness into our lives starts with a step toward Him first and always. What will you ask Him today so that you can get closer to Him forevermore?

* * *

Lord, in Your guidance, I submit to You, asking for direction for my heart that only You can give. I choose to allow You into my life, into the good and the bad, as I learn and grow each day. Thank You for providing the answers I need, for revealing to me how to serve and change, for teaching me **Who You are** *by guiding me closer to You. Amen.*

Part 4

To Rest, to Retreat

He who dwells in the shelter of the Most High
will rest in the shadow of the Almighty.

PSALM 91:1 NIV

Chapter 22

Fighting Insecurity Is Hard Work!

Do you not know? Have you not heard? The LORD is the everlasting God, the Creator of the ends of the earth. He will not grow tired or weary, and his understanding no one can fathom.

ISAIAH 40:28 NIV

Getting to know God is not a task for the lazy among us. It's a full-time job! It's an exquisite journey of wonderful insights and discoveries, but it's not a passive pursuit. We study and ask and test and argue and run and grow—all in the greatest endeavor that produces the greatest bounty: a secure relationship with our Lord.

As we work on that relationship and God unveils to us His glories—as we can understand them—we see everything we learn about Him amassing under us like a giant pillow of love to cradle us when we're tired, to refresh us when we're weary. God's arms faithfully wrap around us and give us refuge from the world. He brings us solace and sanctuary as we grow and learn. He knows we cannot sustain ourselves, so He is here, always, strong enough when we aren't.

✳ ✳ ✳

"I'm so very tired sometimes," I whisper. "There is always some new insecurity crowding around to threaten me. It feels like a constant battle."

"It is, but you are getting stronger every day. And everything you've learned pads a little more the place you fall when an insecurity hits."

"Sometimes I think I can't go on. I'm so tired I can barely form the words to pray."

"That's okay. I know they're there."

"Because You're that smart, right?!"

"Because you're letting Me that close to you, close enough to renew and restore you as much and as often as you need."

"No matter what? No matter where?"

"Of course. I'm never too tired, never far away."

"Please hold me now; help me recover."

"Please know Me now. I am your rest and your retreat forever."

Where can I go from Your Spirit? Or where

*can I flee from Your presence? If I ascend
into heaven, You are there; if I make my
bed in hell, behold, You are there. If I take
the wings of the morning, and dwell in the
uttermost parts of the sea, even there Your
hand shall lead me, and Your right hand
shall hold me.*

PSALM 139:7–10 NKJV

Pausing the Noise

Don't you just wish we could call a time-out from
life every now and then? Wouldn't it be great
to make everything stop while we regained our
strength and refocused our energy?

Well, the world may not be too concerned
with our need for rest, but you can be assured that
the Lord is. He knows when we're heading for
overload even when we don't. And while we may
wonder how to pause the demands and responsibilities upon us, God looks at it another way. He is
close enough to work around the noise, to use
these times we're overwhelmed as teaching tools.

He helps us pause the noise by getting quiet
Himself. If He whispers, we whisper in return. If
He shows us a quiet discovery, we hear Him be-
cause we're concentrating solely on Him. And while

we're doing all that wonderful work we can do no other way, we're at rest.

I know you think that I may need a little rest myself after that comment, that I've tricked you here, because rest can't equal work. But in this case, it does. Here's how.

All in Focus

Working in your rest is work intensely focused. You're too tired to dare, to test, even to ask, so you are stopped and in waiting. And with your attention undivided and your strength depleted, you are still.

All of your resistance and compulsion to do anything your own way subsides. You may appear a passive part of this process, but you're so much more. You're a glass being refilled, a thirsty root system soaking up overdue rains. You look blank, inactive, but you are finding security in God's strength to renew in the rest.

"Be still, and know that I am God," He says (Psalm 46:10 NIV). And in our rest, we are stilled but not stalled. Some of your greatest lessons about *Who God is* will come when you are too tired to do anything but listen and accept what He gives. The Lord's faithfulness makes Him strong enough to reach us and teach us in all our work, even our rest.

The Noise Inside

I think I exhaust myself even more than the world does most of the time. Maybe you do, too. We put a lot of pressure on ourselves, set unreasonable expectations, and then try to squeeze a lesson about God somewhere on the "to-do" list. That's so backward. It's like scrubbing a floor all day with dirty water—you're tired, all right, but you've still got a dirty floor. Your strength is gone, and you're no closer to your goal.

The same kind of dirty water runs round and round our spirits sometimes, too, and that sloshing within gets louder and louder until we must make a choice: We can rely on our strength to quiet it, or we can rely on the Lord's.

> *And He said to me, "My grace is sufficient for you, for My strength is made perfect in weakness."*
>
> 2 CORINTHIANS 12:9 NKJV

Since His strength is perfectly suited to perform flawlessly in my abundant weakness, allowing the Lord to take care of that noise inside is sounding like the better choice every minute, a match made in heaven even! And He cannot fail because "He has girded Himself with strength" (Psalm 93:1 NKJV).

Relying on God's strength means getting to *know* that strength, and it's most evident when we have none of our own, when we are still and quiet, unafraid to trust.

The noise within is scary, but it's just a few weak insecurities. The *Lord* within is faithful, and He will restore us in our rest.

 Chapter 23

Resting from the Fear

Some of the loudest noise within comes from those fears we can't seem to shake, the ones that fatigue us with their pushy ways and garbled logic. We fight them, but when we fight them alone, we lose.

It's easy for our world to become one giant scare when everywhere we turn we see something to hurt us, something to bring harm or hardship into our lives, onto our families. We are consumed by the fear that drains our hearts and makes rest hard to come by.

That exhaustion possesses us when we forget to trust what we know about our Father and His faithfulness, when our very human skepticism stiff-arms us away from His comfort. And in our aloneness, we'll find no security.

What is especially exhausting is to fight the same battles over and over again. The pace takes its toll, and we need to rest. We have only two places to look for it: in God's arms or outside of them.

* * *

"Why do you keep letting the same insecurities frighten you so?" He asks.

"I don't know. They're just so *big.*"

"They feel big because you're letting them defeat you. No wonder you're tired!"

"How can I defeat them instead?"

"With strength. Come and rest a while and renew your strength with Mine."

"Because Your strength is never depleted, is it?"

"And it never will be. My strength fills your soul and will always be what you need, always perfect, always enough, always a part of Me."

> [Jesus] will stand and shepherd his flock in the strength of the LORD, in the majesty of the name of the LORD his God. And they will live securely, for then his greatness will reach to the ends of the earth. And he will be their peace.
>
> MICAH 5:4–5 NIV

The Same Fears

Those repeating fears threaten our rest and our peace. Unlike new struggles, they know us well and prey upon our weaknesses. If you're fighting the same money worries that won't go away, a difficult relationship that doesn't improve, a struggle with a job you don't understand—it's because you're not resting those fears in the faithfulness of God's strength.

Do you think those fears are too big for Him? Of course not, but they *are* too big for us, because these everyday troubles weigh us down and can even turn us away from God when we grant them a long life. Maybe you want to duel it out with those recurring fears once and for all. The advice from God is to be prepared when you do.

> *Therefore put on the full armor of God, so that when the day of evil comes, you may be able to stand your ground, and after you have done everything, to stand.*

EPHESIANS 6:13 NIV

The evils that weaken us may come from within or without, but the preparation for them and the security from them is the same. When we have invested our time and energy in getting to know *Who God is,* we can then rest in the security that His strength provides.

We are like little children lifted high into the air by playful parents. There is no fear in the little one because there is trust that Mom's or Dad's strength will never fail. It is a faithfulness God lives every day, with His arms tender and yet so strong that they can never let us go.

We can learn how to fight the fears that plague us, to do everything that's commanded, and then to "stand" still and secure in the Lord's presence. He prepares us; then He provides a retreat to strengthen us. Our insecurities seek escape because God the Conqueror is here. We just need to remind ourselves, "Yeah, You're still here, Lord. Let's take a breath and regroup."

In our retreat unto God, we can take stock of where we are and review everything we've learned so far. We may be standing still, but we are far from static. And in the midst of the chaos of everyday attacks that are just part of life, a few moments of rest with God is a rescue of our hearts.

He reached down from on high and took hold of me; he drew me out of deep waters. He rescued me from my powerful enemy, from my foes, who were too strong for me. They confronted me in the day of my disaster, but the LORD was my support. He brought me out into a spacious place; he rescued me because he delighted in me.

PSALM 18:16–19 NIV

God the Rescuer

If we're running or fighting or struggling or just suffering the growing pains of a flawed disciple, we find that looking to God for rescue and rest becomes the most normal thing in the world. And lucky for us, He is too faithful to ever leave us stranded and alone.

God the Rescuer saves us from ourselves. When we're too tired or too confused to go on, He rescues us by providing that soft place to fall—His heart that is always strong enough to hold our hurts, no matter how big they are.

We might think rescuing us would be an imposition on the Lord, but no. He is always still here, at the end of our plea, at the beginning of our rest. And if we'll look and listen, we'll see that He wastes nothing. Quiet and still in our retreat, we learn more of *Who He is* and why He has so perfectly designed even our resting time so He can be near us.

Chapter 24

Revelations in the Rest

My flesh and my heart fail; but God is the strength of my heart and my portion forever.

PSALM 73:26 NKJV

Tired bodies and minds scramble our thoughts and interfere with even the most basic parts of our lives. We become supersensitive to other people's comments, to the elements, even to our own actions. We need rest so that we can return to our true selves, so that we can work and play and love with everything we are, holding nothing back.

It's the same with our spirits. When our spirits are tired and depleted, we need that "spacious place" of God's Spirit to recover.

* * *

"I need to know—will You be here when I can barely take a step, when I'm too tired to work?"

"I'm always here, and when you rest in My Spirit, My strengths will be revealed to you."

That soft space between the Lord's arms, close to His heart, welcomes me.

"Please, show me now."

✳ ✳ ✳

In the quiet of a retreat unto God, when we give our fight over to Him, we can get to know those strengths He draws on to support us. We can rebuild and renew because He is faithful to stay with us in our recovery, as long as it takes.

He doesn't stop the world when we need to rest, but it almost feels that way, when we relax into His control and trust His strength to be enough to get us through. The insecurities may be swarming around us like mad wasps, but our peace in the rest is enough to keep them away. When we rely on God to rescue us, He always does because it's part of *Who He is*. His strengths are simple and yet so powerful and perfect. Learning about them is a joy and a renewal tucked away in a retreat, inspiring everything that follows.

When we know His strengths of *character, purpose,* and *truth,* they become ours. And all is well.

> *He gives power to the weak, and to those*
> *who have no might He increases strength.*

ISAIAH 40:29 NKJV

God's Strength of Character

Because the Lord is faithful, He always does the right thing. It's always His only choice.

A television character may debate issues back and forth with the little disproportionate angel on one shoulder and the pitchfork-toting devil on the other. He wonders which path to follow. We laugh, and we do the same thing ourselves nearly every day. But the Lord misses that part of a silly earthling's life.

While our free will allows us to choose, God's strength of character has already made all of His choices for Him. And when we know and claim this great strength for ourselves, we cast aside those insecurities that would make us choose more than once as well. This strength is a part of *Who God is*, not a decision He makes based on each issue's circumstances but a fact that impacts all others.

We get to know the Lord's strength of character well in a state of rest—when we're not trying to accomplish or win or fight, but we're just absorbing His unfailing integrity.

God's character, which keeps Him forever faithful by our side, makes us strong enough to meet anything that would question our own strength. When we begin to feel compromised or pressured, we can do the right thing, too, because He's already made His choice, and we can follow it.

God is so strong that nothing can sway Him from this part of His soul. We can watch that behavior as we rest in Him, as we read about His wisdom, learn from others who have been touched by His grace, and witness His constant care for our broken spirits.

Safe and secure in His arms, we can drink in *Who He is* and let that change *who we are*. Our insecurities shrivel like wilted flowers, and the exhaustion they create in us fades like colors in bright sunlight. Sometimes still, but never alone, we learn that we don't have to worry about new choices that appear every day. In every circumstance we face, in every dilemma, all we have to do is look to see Who's *still* holding us close and claim His strength of character for ourselves.

> *No temptation has overtaken you except such as is common to man; but God is faithful, who will not allow you to be tempted beyond what you are able, but with the temptation will also make the way of escape, that you may be able to bear it.*

1 CORINTHIANS 10:13 NKJV

That "way of escape" that makes us strong enough to bear all temptations—which are feelings of our own making (James 1:14)—is the knowledge of God's character that never falters. If we know how He would choose for us if we allowed Him to, then our choice is suddenly rather uncomplicated.

You can apply any twenty-first-century baggage to any choice that you want, but it doesn't change *Who God is,* and it's no threat to your security when it rests in His strength of character.

Maybe some choices will require a lack of tolerance for something we know is wrong, and we'll need to be like Jesus when He turned over the tables in the temple (John 2:14–16). Or maybe we'll need to have the boldness of the woman at the well (John 4:6–29), or the trust of the woman healed by Jesus' touch (Luke 8:43–48).

Choices like that are not the insecurities they appear to be when we're relying on God's strength of character, and His strength is always here because He knew how much we'd need it. And today and always, His Son, who sympathizes with our weaknesses, also serves as the greatest example of character we could ever look for (Hebrews 4:15).

We don't have to live in a struggle or tire ourselves every day. We can go in confidence, following a path He has already chosen. We can rest in Him and talk to Him and trust in His unchanging character to build our own.

God's Strength of Purpose

What I have said, that will I bring about;
what I have planned, that will I do.

ISAIAH 46:11 NIV

No one can ever accuse the Lord of being a slacker! He is forever loyal to His purpose because He is forever faithful to finish what He starts. He never lets the everyday inconveniences and road-blocks stop His work. How often can we say that about ourselves?

While *the Lord* is never insecure, we wonder all the time if *we* can achieve our purposes and reach our goals, day after day. He understands our frustration with the fights and interruptions and confusion we encounter regularly, and He knows why we need to rest in Him over and over again, weak and insecure. We can tap into God's *strength of purpose* when we ask and allow Him into those encounters.

✳   ✳   ✳

"You need a little while to recuperate from the blows of the world, don't you?"

"How'd You guess?" I sigh.

He laughs. "You have that 'beaten' look, but your insecurities are no match for My strength. Remember?"

"Yes, but I feel too weak to fight the forces that rally against me all the time. I don't know if I'll make it to the finish line."

"That's because you're fighting everything alone, and it exhausts you. I'm here, running along beside you. Don't you want My help?"

"Oh, yes! Will You hold me when my goals are hard to reach, when I need a place to steady myself against all that tires me?"

"Of course. Follow Me, rest in Me, renew *your* strength of purpose by retreating unto *Mine.*"

"And I won't be so tired and unsure?"

"Exactly, because you will be sure of *Me.* I will never abandon you in our work. Rest in that promise."

* * *

What a comfort it is to know that God will always be here, even when I stray from my path, when I feel like giving up, when the discouragement is too strong for me to bear. All of that fatigue is countered with the strength of God on a mission.

Knowing that brings a rest that can prepare us to rejoin the challenges we face. God's strength of purpose will not wane because it's part of *Who He is.* And He makes it available to us, to become another part of who we are, too.

I will bless the LORD who has given me counsel; my heart also instructs me in the night seasons. I have set the LORD always before me; because He is at my right hand I shall not be moved.

PSALM 16:7–8 NKJV

Sometimes when we're tired and discouraged about our lives, we lose all hope and interest in what the Lord has called us to do. We may look for excuses for our behavior or ways to justify our poor choices, but all we really need is a shift in focus.

If we constantly just look for benchmarks or dollar signs, we'll miss the point. Achieving our lives' purposes isn't just about reaching a tangible goal—it's about paying attention to Who's journeying with us. His first purpose is always to be close to us. Then all other purposes follow.

That's why God's strength of purpose is so remarkable. He can do "whatever He pleases," (Psalm 115:3 NKJV), and He pleases first to be faithful to our need, to be strong when we are weak, to let us retreat unto Him so that we can remember our grandest purpose, too—knowing *Who He is.*

God's Strength of Truth

*God is not a man, that he should lie, nor a
son of man, that he should change his
mind. Does he speak and then not act?
Does he promise and not fulfill?*

NUMBERS 23:19 NIV

"Why do I lose and confuse the truth sometimes?"

"Because you give in to fear, and that tires
you and pulls you away from Me."

"What can I do instead?"

"You can choose to trust what is real, what
I've told you about *Who I am.* In that, you will
always find great strength of truth."

"And then what happens?"

"You have the strength to demand only the truth
in everything you do. Nothing is harder than working on a lie. When you know the truth, tell the truth,
and live the truth, you make your world an easier
place to navigate. And in that truth, you'll find Me."

"And I can do that because You can't lie to me,
can You?"

"Lying definitely isn't a part of *Who I am!*"

"Tell me something once, and I can hold it
forever, right?"

"Right. I am faithful to My word, so that you
can be, too."

Promised Security

Do you know what one of the most tiring things you can do to yourself is? We don't even usually realize it, but if we lie to ourselves, we'll certainly recognize the effect: complete exhaustion. We lie to ourselves either by denying who we are or by denying *Who God is*. The result is a life that is only a constant chore, a way of living that ignores God's strength of truth and all that it gives us. The result is insecurity.

These falsehoods, or insecurities, in your life happen when you allow yourself to be talked into something that doesn't fit with who you are—with your strength of *character* or *purpose*. They happen when you reject God's claims and powers, telling yourself that He's not big enough or caring enough for what you need. They happen when you accept anything into your life that isn't based on your knowledge of God.

And lying or accepting lies steals great peace and joy from your heart and soul. It's like running in waist-deep mud in the dark, holding your breath. You can't see, and you can't find any rest—only a deep hole in your heart where God wants to live. The lies are getting closer, and you can't run any faster. Stop trying to run in a lie, and instead, let God restore your strength to accept the truth that originates in Him.

If He speaks to you or promises you or teaches you or touches you—there is no need to doubt that He will follow through. Know that, and be secure. Because He sees great strength in the truth, so can we. It's another choice He made once, and it's one we can make forever because of Him. It would never occur to the Lord to lie! The truth is so much a great part of *Who He is* that it is the basis for one of mankind's greatest stories.

> *For when God made a promise to Abraham, because He could swear by no one greater, He swore by Himself, saying, "Surely blessing I will bless you, and multiplying I will multiply you."*
>
> HEBREWS 6:13–14 NKJV

Abraham believed with a strength of truth and faith we want for ourselves. And in his most fearful moment, he was met by his most faithful God, unfailingly honest to *Who He is,* at a time far more dramatic than most of our everyday catastrophes.

If the Lord was true to that strength then, He is true to it today, able to take any faith we offer up to Him and bless us with it indeed. And that's a revelation to hold forever.

Chapter 25

Retreating to Recharge

How has the Lord met you and challenged you in your life? Has He placed ideas and goals upon your heart and kick-started you in the right direction? Have you felt His push to be the disciple He needs? Do you know exactly what the work is that He has planned for you?

All the work that we do *for* God shows us more *about* God. We see Him at work in our lives, too, in great and small ways. Some days are just like one big hug from Him when we know we're going in the right direction and we hear Him perfectly. I'm sure He's completely capable of making every day like that for us, if we'll allow it.

But we don't have His perfect strength, and we lose our steam now and then. We feel a chink in our conviction. We hit a few obstacles and feel insecure about the inspiration we once so boldly claimed. And we wonder if God is feeling a little less than inspired with us at the same time. That *never* happens, because He never gives up on us, but He understands well our inconsistent drive and fearful enthusiasm.

That's when He takes us close and reminds us of His everlasting love, when He invites us to retreat to the strength and security of His soul, when we delight again and again in His attention.

> *Be merciful to me, O God, be merciful to*
> *me! For my soul trusts in You; and in the*
> *shadow of Your wings I will make my*
> *refuge, until these calamities have passed by.*

PSALM 57:1 NKJV

* * *

"Lord, where are You when I'm feeling less than inspired and motivated about everything You've poured into my life?"

"You know that answer by now."

"Yes, I do. You're *still here,* but so is my restlessness. And I'm too tired to fight it now."

"You don't have to fight these experiences. We can use them instead."

"I don't see how. Are You looking at this mess? I'm wasting so much time."

"Never. Nothing is wasted. Instead of trying so very hard to go when you can't, stop and retreat unto Me, and we will just be together. That's always enough."

So, He *is* looking. Now I can draw a restful breath.

Retreating from the Insecurities

Every time we go to God tired and spent, we carry several insecurities with us, those not yet tested or those we need to test again. Sometimes it's a feeling of inadequacy or disappointment. I've felt that way when my career would seem to be vanishing like smoke, as if it never happened. But in the safety of a retreat unto God, I could talk to Him about all that bothered and beat me. And He would always be here to listen so that I could learn.

Maybe you know that kind of retreat. The Lord will meet us there anytime, for a short stay or a long one, whatever we need. Sometimes we may only need to sit still a little while and pray our weariness away—finding renewed enthusiasm, comfort, and strength in Him.

At other times, we may need to learn some new wonders about the Lord's faithfulness that we've missed before or accept a new blessing He wants to give us to help us carry on. The retreat the Lord prepares for us will be the exact duration that we need, because it's part of *Who He is.*

On some of those days when my work was hard, when I wondered about the significance of it all, I've needed to retreat to God's significance, to ask Him to help me through the quiet times when my impatient, earthly soul needed something I could touch, evidence that my steps were in the right direction.

And even when the questions in my mind were loud, God would stay close, comforting me in the quiet and helping me define my life on *His* terms, helping me lean on *His* judgment and trust in *His* timing. If I asked for more direction, sometimes He'd tell me I was asking to see too far, and He would remind me to rest a moment where I was, to look around before looking ahead.

He would comfort and inspire me with His command of my situation—no matter how small it was compared to the big things He had to deal with. He always has the time to hold us tightly, to remind us of His presence, still where we looked for Him last. He generously gives us the desire to start again.

God's faithfulness to His purpose for our lives includes His attention to us when we're stalled, flat, or confused. His strength to restore us is another part of *Who He is*—and why He will never leave us alone. He monitors our progress, and sometimes He even stops it for a very good reason.

 Chapter 26

When God Says "Rest"

The Lord's power just never ends. He is so intuitive, so sure of everything we need to be the disciple *He* needs. When we forsake the rest we need, He often decides for us, and we stop and rest because it is His good judgment that we do so.

Sometimes, God stops us from our busyness and brings us to Him for no other reason than to be with us, to train our focus where it should be. We may fail to recognize the reasons at first, but we know the drill: We are stopped in our tracks when God says, *"It's time to talk to Me a while."* It comes when we haven't a clue what to do next after doing so very much, and He says, "Rest." Our busyness stops so that we can catch up.

Our retreat brings more knowledge of *Who God is* when we're listening instead of talking, resting instead of doing. It's not laziness or reluctance to work—just a time-out when God blows the whistle, a quiet change of pace that reveals its own discoveries. Get quiet and listen. . . . Hold on to what you hear.

> *I will meditate on Your precepts, and contemplate Your ways. I will delight myself in Your statutes; I will not forget Your word.*

> PSALM 119:15–16 NKJV

A Rest in God

God says, *"Rest in Me"* when we're so absorbed in all our work that we forget about our relationship with the strongest Worker of all, when we dismiss or disallow His work in our lives. That's when the weight of the world comes down on us—when we feel discouraged, depressed, or disconnected from God and all that's good. Our response is a little off.

We isolate ourselves and figure that if we just work a little harder we'll get where we're trying to go. We analyze and dissect everything around us, applying the same workhorse mentality to our spirits that we force onto our bodies and minds when there's too much work to be done. The result is collapse, still kicking but never moving, because there is nothing to fuel our fires.

When we don't go back to God for the sustenance and pause we need to get a handle on what's true and what matters, we lose our strength and our focus. He knows when our spirit is troubled, exhausted, and in special need of Him. Those are the times when He says, *"Wait a minute. You're getting way off track, falling away from Me as you work at such a pace. Come here; let's rest a moment."*

That's when everything seems to stop no matter what you do. That's when you have that familiar pull to go back to where you started, to shove away the irritating strikes to your will, to rest in the basics, when nothing more than "God loves me" can get through. And that's where God's waiting, faithful to gently correct your way and softly cradle your spirit, when your "stilled and quieted" soul (Psalm 131:2 NIV) surrenders to His rest.

✷ ✷ ✷

"I've been working really hard," I tell Him. Maybe there are points for that somewhere.

"I know, but you try to do too much alone."

That didn't sound like points to me. I'll try again.

"But it's tough here in the flesh! The realities and deadlines of my world pain and burden me!"

"Of course they do, when you face them alone. Don't worry. You will find your way to serve everywhere you're needed, but not without a regular rest in *Me.*"

"It seems backward—to stop so that I may go."

"But you're never stopped when your spirit is engaging Mine. You are at rest so that you can replenish your strength, so that you can learn again to lean unto Me for all the support you will ever need."

"And You won't let go of me?"

"Not a chance. I hold you close because it's part of *Who I am,* your haven from the hurt so that you may heal."

* * *

Ah, I love that part, too! To know that my going about my busyness achieves nothing if I have not stopped first is to know that God is looking out for me, that He values my spiritual health and will save me from myself, again and again.

And as comforting as this knowledge is, there have been other times when I've felt the need for a rest in God—and wondered if He would allow it. My worries were always unfounded, though, because He is as forgiving as He is faithful.

"What about now?" I ask.

And His response is always the same.

> *"Come to me, all you who are weary and burdened, and I will give you rest. Take my yoke upon you and learn from me, for I am gentle and humble in heart, and you will find rest for your souls."*

MATTHEW 11:28–29 NIV

Chapter 27

A Repentant Retreat

For He knows our frame;
He remembers that we are dust.

PSALM 103:14 NKJV

One of the most beautiful and effective ways to know God is to experience His grace. We are never more in need of a retreat unto Him than when we need His forgiveness and redemption. And no matter what, every time we ask, He says, *"Now is fine."*

Look at everything that's wrong in my life. Can I give this to You? we plead.

"Now is fine," He says.

I've been distant and disobedient. Can I return to You?

"Now is fine," He says.

I'm so lost and so tired. Can I rest in You?

"Now is fine," He says.

There is no time, no issue, no past that will keep us away from God one second longer than we want it to. As soon as we ask Him to be here, to repair and renew us, He says yes. The timing is perfect as soon as we breathe one request for a retreat unto Him, "not because of anything we have done but because of his own purpose and grace" (2 Timothy 1:9 NIV).

And in His arms, what do we find? Ridicule? No. Anger? No. We find the Lord who has loved us through every mistake, completely and unquestionably faithful to His promise of redemption, strong enough to save us by His grace. We can't buy it or earn it. We can only ask humbly for it and allow Him to deliver. "Thanks be to God for His indescribable gift!" (2 Corinthians 9:15 NKJV).

* * *

"I love to give to you," He says, "and that includes My grace."

"I am undeserving."

"And I am compassionate. I dispense My grace to those who *need* it. It is My gift. It is My soul."

"But I am still weak and quite likely to mess up again."

"And I am strong and will still be here when

you need My grace again."

He smiled with that comment and watched my face reveal the dawning in my mind of its significance couched in understatement.

Well, of course He would still be here to rest me through every misstep. What did I think He was anyway—unfaithful to His word or too weak to honor it? Sometimes only in a rest do we allow the obvious to penetrate our walled hearts and rescue us with its power.

Let us therefore come boldly to the throne of grace, that we may obtain mercy and find grace to help in time of need.

HEBREWS 4:16 NKJV

Just Like God

"Don't You ever get tired of my constant needs? I'm sorry to be so much trouble."

"Oh, My child, your life is a process. Anything that draws you closer to Me is never tiresome. And when you *need* Me, you get to *know* Me. That's what *I* need. Come, rest; let Me bless you again and always."

How like God—to welcome us to His heart when we have walked away. He grants us a retreat from our past and repairs us for the future. He is faithful to always answer our call for His grace, and if that isn't enough, there's even a bonus in the gift.

In our rest, we can pause and rejoice in the Lord's willingness to accept us and love us and carry us through the terribly difficult times in our lives. He doesn't waste even our times of repentance, when we feel stagnant and ashamed. In fact, much is going on in our deceptively still view because "inwardly we are being renewed day by day" (2 Corinthians 4:16 NIV).

The times of rest renew us with newfound knowledge—about God and ourselves. We learn to know His strong and gentle hand that guides us nearer to Him, and we learn how our mistakes can only be forgiven by God and then transformed into something He can use.

In the strength of His grace, we reaffirm our belief that we are capable of accomplishing anything He asks of us, even when we stray and lose our way sometimes. He will forever be right here, still, to guide us back to where we need to be and to refresh us along the way, so that we may "go in the strength of the Lord GOD" (Psalm 71:16 NKJV).

We learn that the purposes of our lives remain

even when we fail. We rest and regain our strength to bear the fruit of our Lord's choosing.

> *"I am the vine, you are the branches. He who abides in Me, and I in him, bears much fruit; for without Me you can do nothing."*

JOHN 15:5 NKJV

 Chapter 28

After the Rest

Return to your rest, O my soul,
for the LORD has dealt bountifully with you.

PSALM 116:7 NKJV

"Lord, You're a genius!"

"You think so?"

"Yes! Not only do You grant Your grace without end, uphold me with Your strength, and restore my focus when I lose my way, but You never fail to give me something I can carry with me *after* my rest."

"Like what?"

"When You forgive me, I learn forgiveness for others. And when You hold me in my state of shame, I learn compassion and humility. When You teach me Your great strengths, I can make them mine and be more like You every day. Then after a warm retreat unto You, I feel strong enough to take on the world again with more confidence and security than I've ever known before."

"I give you what you need. It's that simple."

"It's that *perfect!* How'd You get to be so smart?"

"Practice," He says with a twinkle.

✳ ✳ ✳

Okay, so the Lord has had to rescue me a few more times than the average soul, but there's no need to worry. He's *still here* with me when I lose my way, when I lose His way, and when I simply have no way to keep going. He's still there with you, too.

My weaknesses are well known to Him (and my family, too—just ask them), but as He rescues me from those weaknesses, His strengths become a part of me. Nothing is wasted.

The rest is for a reason, the retreat a response of His faithfulness.

> *Create in me a clean heart, O God, and renew a steadfast spirit within me. Do not cast me away from Your presence, and do not take Your Holy Spirit from me.*

> PSALM 51:10–11 NKJV

✳ ✳ ✳

God's faithfulness is God's strength. *He says to me, "There is nothing in you that My strength cannot reach. I am your rest from the blows of this world and your return to the journey we travel together, forever strong enough to rescue and redeem you in one heartbeat.* ***That strength is*** *Who I am."*

To Rest, To Retreat—in God's Strength

- How do you go to God when you're tired? Do you let Him rescue you or do you question His strength to do so?

- What fears exhaust you over and over? How can you put those fears to rest in a retreat unto the Lord?

- Have you ever learned about any of God's great strengths during a rest? How have you made them your own?

- When have you needed to retreat unto the Lord to recharge and renew your spirit? How did He respond, and how will you accept those retreats in the future?

- How have you reacted when God has told you to rest? Did you allow yourself to learn anything about Him or yourself during those times?

- How have you been afraid to rest in the Lord after a failure? How has He responded to your cries?
- Do you see that nothing is wasted, that times of action and inaction are all times of learning? What have your rests taught you about the Lord's faithfulness?

✳   ✳   ✳

Lord, in Your strength, *I find rest for my soul, a retreat where I'm safe and secure. Please help me to appreciate the times of rest in my life and to learn of Your strengths of character, purpose, and truth. Then after my rest, I will know more about* **Who You are** *as I claim the strength of Your faithfulness to remain. Amen.*

Part 5

To Know, to Go

Oh, the depth of the riches both of the wisdom and knowledge of God!

ROMANS 11:33 NKJV

Chapter 29

Knowing in the Dark

Forever faithful to His promises, through all our doubting and daring and testing and asking, the Lord stays with us without one complaint. And then, when we're exhausted and off course, He gives us rest and teaches us even more in a secure retreat. His patience truly is remarkable, and through everything, we come heart to heart with His love and power and guidance and strength. Through everything, He is faithful. He is still here. Our insecurity dies as our knowledge grows.

And finally, we begin to see that not one step of our journey is by accident! Nothing is unplanned or unscripted. Somehow, in some way, God knows everything we'll need, every question we'll ask, every struggle we'll endure. He is never surprised or unprepared for our insecurity. His supply meets our every lack, His provision our every emptiness.

Like watching a flower bloom in lapsed time,

we're aware of a plan far grander than we could ever grasp. And we're enveloped in the Master Planner's wisdom, encased in the soft petals of His love. "Amazing" seems too tame a word for His command of our lives, the blessing of knowing Him intimately too great to be described.

✳ ✳ ✳

"I'm learning. I'm slow sometimes, Lord, but I'm learning. And knowing You makes my insecurity vanish!"

"I know. That's the plan," He says to me.

"Well, You'll forgive me if I came to that conclusion a little late? I don't have Your infinite wisdom, You know." I thought maybe He'd forgotten just how limited I am.

"Yes, you do."

Huh? I had Him this time, though.

"Wait a minute. No one knows as much as You do. No one can."

"And you don't have to."

Well, now, I was thoroughly confused and felt as wise as candle wax.

"I'm afraid I need a little clarification here, Lord. How can You say I have Your wisdom and then say I don't need to know as much as You do?" (I wanted to see Him get out of this one!)

"Easy. Because I'm a part of you, and you're a part of Me. Understand?"

Clear as tree bark. I wonder if this little puzzle is some of that "fun" part He promised a while back. . . ?

God, a Part of Me

Sometimes I've wondered why the Lord would *want* to be a part of me, to dwell in my heart and bless me endlessly, but I've learned not to question His motives, just to enjoy His faithfulness and devotion instead. It was *His* idea to love me beyond reason, I remember.

> *The LORD is faithful to all his promises*
> *and loving toward all he has made.*
>
> PSALM 145:13 NIV

And the result is as perfect as He promised: no insecurity! That's because my security is all wrapped up in knowing *Who He is,* and those lessons only come when He's living in my heart, still, always.

I learn about His character, His habits, and His strengths. And if I truly *know* Him, I *trust* Him. And as we journey together to the edge of every jagged cliff my life leads me to, I learn to follow His example. I grow and I change and I find security and peace and—yes!—wisdom that comes from knowing *Who He is.*

Through the love of God and the life of Christ "in whom are hidden all the treasures of wisdom and knowledge" (Colossians 2:3 NKJV), I can claim the same when my heart makes them a home.

No Ego Trip

This wisdom like the Lord's isn't the know-it-all kind of ego that makes people who are too full of themselves intensely annoying. It's a wisdom of reverence and awe and love and trust in the Lord Who will never leave us. It's a wisdom that knows God is *still* here and *still* in charge and quite capable of handling any test or dare we give Him. It's a wisdom in an unlimited God Who blesses us without reason and guides us without fault.

> *The fear of the LORD is the beginning of wisdom.*
>
> PSALM 111:10 NKJV

While He watches over the whole universe and all of our troubles, too, He comes to dwell in our hearts, still teaching us, still touching us, still granting us His wisdom, still knowing what we don't.

Me, a Part of God

So we fix our eyes not on what is seen, but on what is unseen. For what is seen is temporary, but what is unseen is eternal.

2 CORINTHIANS 4:18 NIV

In His grace, the Lord becomes a part of me so that I won't be afraid and insecure. And in His love, He calls me to be a part of Him so that I will trust His voice and follow His Word, when I can see and when I can't. He lives in my heart to grant me wisdom about the choices of my life. I live in His so I can entrust to Him those choices I can't control.

Well, it looks like the Lord *did* know what He was talking about (big surprise, huh?). I can trust myself and the wisdom God has given me, and I can trust *His* wisdom because I know He is faithful to His word.

My human capacity to meet my challenges is limited now and then, but God's isn't. When it's dark and I can't see, I can still go. I can do all I know and then trust what I know best: *Who God is.* No insecurity can withstand that power.

*He has made the earth by His power, He
has established the world by His wisdom,
and has stretched out the heavens at His
discretion.*

JEREMIAH 10:12 NKJV

Chapter 30

Not Knowing Is Okay, Too

Having all the answers is wonderful, isn't it? Making a plan, working out all the details, getting everything in line, and then seeing it all come together with no surprises is a joy indeed. We feel so sure and capable when that happens.

Then there are the times a lot closer to real life—and that's about 99 percent of them, in my case. Those are the times when a plan is an afterthought, the only details I have worked out are "start" and "finish," and the only parts that come together are the broken ones I pick up and throw in a pile. The biggest surprise of all is that I survive. Ever have one of those fun moments?

If we allowed those less-than-perfect times to define our lives, we'd need to catalog our insecurities at the Smithsonian. Fortunately, the Lord still has the world in the palm of His hand, even when we wreck our little acre of it. He is wise and we are rescued by His faithfulness.

* * *

"I think I understand Your answer now," I venture.

"I'm not surprised. You know Me so well."

"Yes, isn't it great?! But despite Your best efforts to educate me and strengthen me and even make me wise like You, there is still so much I don't know, so many times I'm afraid of the edge of the cliff. But even then, I'm not insecure. You know why?"

"Tell Me."

"Because I don't have to know everything when I know *You.*"

"Sounds like I've heard that somewhere before." He winks and smiles.

I do the same.

Knowing That First Step

I love lists, don't you? They are so logical and comforting. Write a list, and you know what to do, what's expected, and what's next. It's a great plan when it works, but guess what? Our real lives don't come with many reliable lists. Amazingly again, the Lord does! Even when we know nothing else, we know where to start. When we know the beginning, all that matters will follow.

> *"This is the work of God, that you believe in Him whom He sent."*
>
> JOHN 6:29 NKJV

When we believe, our world is manageable, and in His faithfulness, God shows us how. When we don't know *exactly* how we'll get through the illness or the betrayal or the abandonment, that's okay, because we know we're not going to go through it alone.

We can rest in the security that God has a handle on the situation, that He's made His list, and we needn't worry. In His wisdom, He gave us a Savior not to fight wars or amass fortunes but to hold hands and mend hurts. At the top of our list is to *believe* that He's still here with us, and at the top of His is to be faithful to still be here no matter what. Great plan, huh?

*   *   *

"Lord, You know my challenges better than I do, and You know my need for You to be here, still, always. Sometimes, all I do know is just to keep believing."

"You make that sound like so little! Believe and know; trust and be secure. And all will become clear."

✱ ✱ ✱

I so want that security! And yet sometimes nothing seems clear in this messy world of mine. I imagine the Lord sitting patiently, waiting for me to stop trying so hard to see ahead and realize what is right in front of me—*Him.* I don't need to see any further than my salvation to deal with these problems my life creates. He generously shares His unfailing wisdom when I ask, and yet everything I need to know to fight my troubles is still back there, the first item on my list and the only one I really need, because it covers everything else.

> *Who is it that overcomes the world? Only he who believes that Jesus is the Son of God.*
>
> 1 JOHN 5:5 NIV

It's logical and linear and wise, and we can write it as a list if we want:

- Believe that God's love and faithfulness was demonstrated when He sent us His Son, Jesus Christ.
- Believe that our security lies in knowing God and knowing how He has provided for us through Christ.
- Believe that we can go about our work

as He would have us, knowing Him and learning through Christ.

- Believe that we can do our work even in a sometimes difficult world because God was faithful to send us His Son, Jesus Christ.

Oops, maybe it's a circle instead of a line! No matter—we still know what we need to know when our belief is in the right place. And then the rest is easier.

The Next Step

"When you don't know anything, you still know everything," God says in His way I've grown accustomed to.

Heavy sigh.

"Did You ever think of writing fortune cookies or something?"

He's amused by my lack of understanding.

"You know what I mean. Think. What did you learn about Me first?"

"That You love me more than anything."

"Exactly. And if I love you, I have given you the same love to guide you. You cannot walk in darkness if you walk in the wisdom of My love."

"But how will I *know?*"

"When you love Me back."

✳ ✳ ✳

Having the wisdom to step forward in love isn't about knowing the path like a Boy Scout knows a topographical map. Even if I have to jump off the cliff *knowing nothing,* I will learn because God will be faithful to teach me as I go *if* I already *know everything*—His love that catches me. My belief makes all the work that comes after it make sense. I can't take a wrong next step if I step with a love for God. It's just not possible.

How wise of the Lord to teach us the most important lesson first! Knowing Him means loving Him means knowing Him. Who needs a list?

 **Chapter 31**

Knowing God, Knowing Yourself

We say, "I want to know You, Lord." And He says, *"Sure, ask Me anything."* We say, "I want to know myself, too." And He says, *"Sure, I've told you everything."*

How can that be? It sounds like another riddle, and yet He's right, of course. We know what we need to know about ourselves because of the stories He's told us through His Son. And if there's anything we don't understand, the Lord will be faithful to explain it to us.

> *If any of you lacks wisdom, he should ask God, who gives generously to all without finding fault, and it will be given to him.*
>
> JAMES 1:5 NIV

If we know God, He grants us the wisdom to know ourselves as the beloved and secure children we are. The abundant life He promises surrounds us like the ocean on a wave—we are one with God, and everything then becomes doable, every place reachable.

We can know and go where He leads because He will always lead us to a place that fits who we are because He knew us first. Becoming closer and closer to our faithful God reveals everything we need to know to live the life He's designed for us.

Knowing the Security

The security we find as we get to know and trust God is the same security we find as we get to know and trust ourselves, because it comes from God. When we learn to trust God to be faithful to us all the time, we discover the courage to be faithful to *who we are in God* all the time.

We accept the free will He gives us, and we take responsibility for our choices. And then we make those choices with better information: the knowledge of God and His plan for our lives.

That's another amazing fact about the Lord—He's in the details. He knows your every thought and wish and secret. He knows how to guide and direct you to the life that fits the special and unique daughter that you are. Nothing is outside His interest, and no circumstance leaves Him unprepared. The stories to teach us about ourselves are already there, in the teachings of Jesus.

* * *

"What if those stories of characters long ago don't apply to my computerized and digitized life, Lord?"

"Impossible."

"You sound pretty sure about that."

"I know how to suspend planets, grow mountains, and fit two hundred bones together so that you can swim like a fish. Don't you think I can handle a few stories?"

"Okay, so *Your* wisdom isn't the problem. What about mine?"

"Trust Me, child," He says, and I can feel Him close. "You never go alone, in this journey inside or any journey outside."

* * *

What makes me think that this "inside" journey may be one of the trickiest of all? I feel so inadequate much of the time, so unable to be the disciple my God needs me to be. Maybe the journey to know Him will help me find Him within myself, sustaining me and supporting me when I begin to question my value. How can I, plain and quite unremarkable, walk with the wisdom of God? How can I give to this world something that matters? And where will I find myself, in those long-ago stories of Jesus' teachings?

I hope the Lord is planning on holding my hand tightly on this leap. It should be one for the books.

Wanting to Be More

You are precious to God, an individual with a sacred calling. But you are also like me and your friends and those people you don't know. We're all struggling to know ourselves and believe in ourselves enough to carry on in a challenging world. And we can succeed because God is faithful to provide everything we need even before we need it.

Everything to help us become what we want to become is already here. In His wisdom, God has given us the food we need to nourish our weak and insecure souls, all in the lives of those who lived many years ago yet hungered for the same basic things we do—how to know God and go forth as He calls.

As you ready yourself for living a secure life in God, you must know yourself the way God knows you. You are His child, loved and wanted. And you are so much more.

You are **redeemed** (John 8:1–11).
We all know this story. A woman is brought before Jesus, and the Pharisees want to see if He will condone stoning her for her sins. His response is unexpected, and His focus is on redemption, not punishment. The accusers scatter, and the woman is left alone with Jesus.

"Go and sin no more," He tells her (John 8:11 NKJV). And so He tells you and me. We see ourselves in that woman, guilty of some transgression, no doubt, standing face-to-face with our Savior and yet unthreatened. If you are to know yourself, you must know that you are forgiven and redeemed, encouraged and brave because of the Lord's faithfulness. *And redeemed, you are secure.*

You are **capable** (Matthew 14:22–33).
Jesus knew His disciples in the boat were in troubled waters, literally. Perhaps without a boat Himself, Jesus walked on the water to be near them. Peter wanted to join Him.

So He said, "Come" (Matthew 14:29 NKJV). With one word, Peter did the impossible because it meant getting him closer to his Lord. All we have to do is ask today, and we are with Him over troubled waters of our own. Peter became scared, and

Jesus caught him. If we become scared, He'll do the same for us. If you are to know yourself, you must know that you are competent and capable, empowered and safe because of the Lord's faithfulness. *And capable, you are secure.*

You are **enabled** (John 5:1–15).
The sick and the lame gathered around the healing pool at Bethesda, hoping to be made well if they could step into the stirring waters quickly enough. One man who had not walked for thirty-eight years was never first into the pool, but he caught the attention of Jesus.

"Rise, take up your bed and walk," Jesus ordered the man, and he was made well immediately (John 5:8 NKJV). Jesus tells us to "rise," too, when we think we're unable. Then He challenges us to use our new power and strength for a better life (verse 14). The healing pool we need today is the heart of Jesus. If you are to know yourself, you must know that you are healed and enabled, inspired and renewed because of the Lord's faithfulness. *And enabled, you are secure.*

You are **directed** (Matthew 28:16–20).
On a mountaintop in Galilee, Jesus talked to His disciples. On a bench in your backyard, He talks to you.

"Go therefore and make disciples. . .teaching

them to observe all things that I have commanded you; and lo, I am with you always," Jesus says then and now (Matthew 28:19–20 NKJV). Because He has taught us, we can teach others. Because He directs us, we know where to go. Because He loves us, we never go alone. If you are to know yourself, you must know that you are challenged and directed, accompanied and able because of the Lord's faithfulness. *And directed, you are secure.*

You are **blessed** (Luke 10:25–37).
I've seen myself as the poor man who was the victim of thieves in the story of the Good Samaritan more than once, and the Lord has sent kind souls to rescue me. And in all He's given me, the same capacity for sharing lives.

"Go and do likewise," Jesus says so simply (Luke 10:37 NKJV). Because I don't travel this journey alone, you and I are likely to meet. Who knows which one of us will be in need at the time? It doesn't matter, because we are both so blessed with a Lord who meets all our needs so that we can "go and do likewise" in the earthly ways we have. Nothing is by chance. If you are to know yourself, you must know that you are adored and blessed, compassionate and whole because of the Lord's faithfulness. *And blessed, you are secure.*

"I will not forget you! See, I have engraved you on the palms of my hands."

ISAIAH 49:15–16 NIV

A Journey Blessed

Whatever you are today, you will be more tomorrow. Whatever your heart needs, the Lord will supply in abundance. It doesn't matter if you need redemption or if you feel incapable, if you have failed before or lost your way. You have within you now the capacity to overcome everything because of the Lord's unending blessings that have come over you.

The great opportunities await, and you will be sent wherever God needs you to be. So keep watch! Look for the chances to be who you are for God. There's no need to look back or dwell on a past that failed to honor Him. Your present and your future are held in your belief in Christ where you are "a new creation; old things have passed away; behold, all things have become new" (2 Corinthians 5:17 NKJV). Step there, on the new, strong and secure. Love Him back.

Our journeys are not a competition. There's no race to see which one of us can know God the best or the quickest. Your journey is a discovery of all that God is and all that you can become because of His faithfulness to you. Know Him, know yourself; then tell others.

> *The law of the LORD is perfect, reviving the soul. The statutes of the LORD are trustworthy, making wise the simple.*

PSALM 19:7 NIV

 Chapter 32

Banking the Knowledge

"I want to hold on to all that You've taught me about You and myself. I know then that there's no way I can be insecure."

"And you can never be without. I'm like an account with an unlimited balance."

"That's something I can't quite relate to, Lord."

He finds my human understanding funny.

"Fair enough," He says. "But in My case, you don't have to dream or imagine. I hold everything, and it's all yours."

"Tell me more."

"Make room for more."

✳ ✳ ✳

"Do not store up for yourselves treasures on earth, where moth and rust destroy, and where thieves break in and steal. But store up for yourselves treasures in heaven, where moth and rust do not destroy, and where

*thieves do not break in and steal. For
where your treasure is, there your heart
will be also."*

Treasures of the Heart

Nothing here on earth can match the security of
God's love, of His promise to be here with us,
still and always. No depository could ever hold
His blessings given freely, and yet He keeps
pouring them daily into our hearts. We hold
those treasures there, a witness to the Lord's faithfulness. And they are treasures of the most deli-
cious kind!

Everything God teaches us about Himself is
something that will guide us through the trials of
our lives. Everything He reveals to us stretches our
minds so that we can apply His faithfulness everywhere we need it. We love Him the more we know
Him, and the more we know Him, the better
equipped we are to go where He sends us. He
knows we lack the wisdom to carry out our purposes on our own, so He gives us His when we ask.

The faith we need to go is found in the treasures we've come to know—by knowing *Who God
is.* These treasures are revealed to us over and over

in three ways: *project, place,* and *circumstance.* We can test our every action against what we know about God, and He will give us the wisdom to go about our work. The account is full, and it always will be.

Treasures of Project

Nehemiah wanted to rebuild the walls of Jerusalem that were destroyed in battle, and he prayed to God for the chance. He probably didn't pray for the frustration and opposition that came with the project, but he never gave up, even when his safety was at stake.

Governors of the surrounding territories feared the progress of Nehemiah and his followers. They mocked him: "Will they restore their wall? . . . Will they finish in a day? . . . What they are building— if even a fox climbed up on it, he would break down their wall of stones!" (Nehemiah 4:2–3 NIV). Nehemiah was unmoved, and he just kept building.

Then they threatened him, but Nehemiah prayed and prepared. "They all plotted together to come and fight against Jerusalem and stir up trouble against it. But we prayed to our God and posted a guard day and night to meet this threat"

(Nehemiah 4:8–9 NIV).

Then the laborers were tired and afraid, knee-deep in debris as they tried to work. Nehemiah comforted them, reminded them of God's faithfulness, and organized them to be "guards by night and workmen by day" (Nehemiah 4:22 NIV). Despite the threat of war and the fatigue of the crew, Nehemiah completed the work the Lord had given him to do. He was wise and compassionate, strong and secure, and in fifty-two days, he rebuilt the walls of Jerusalem.

Nehemiah worked on the knowledge stored in his heart, on his faith in God. He knew that despite obstacles and setbacks, the Lord's work would be done. He knew that as long as he kept doing his part the best he knew how, the project would be complete. God blessed Nehemiah with a *treasure of project*—a way to grow even closer to Him and know even more about Him, and we can have the same.

Nehemiah was given a project that matched his wisdom and faith. You have an account of those projects in God's plan, too. Your account holds all of the great treasures that God wants to reveal to you in your day-to-day life. We'll probably not be called upon to build a wall, but maybe we'll build a friendship or a flower garden. Your projects are just as noble as Nehemiah's was when they're done hand in hand with the Lord. Don't ever think you can't go where you feel led. You've learned so much, and you're so prepared. Go, and carry along an extra bag for all the treasures you're about to receive!

> *I know that whatever God does, it shall be forever. Nothing can be added to it, and nothing taken from it. God does it, that men should fear before Him.*
>
> ECCLESIASTES 3:14 NKJV

Treasures of Place

When Ruth chose to go to a foreign land, she didn't make that choice alone. That was a pretty big cliff she stepped off of, but she leapt with all the faith she had. And once she chose to go to Bethlehem with her mother-in-law, Naomi, she never looked back.

> *"Entreat me not to leave you, or to turn back from following after you; for wherever you go, I will go; and wherever you lodge, I will lodge; your people shall be my people, and your God, my God."*
>
> RUTH 1:16 NKJV

Even if Ruth was afraid of living in a foreign place, she was more afraid of denying her faith and her wisdom to make the decision she did. She knew that the rest of her life depended on that choice, and she trusted God to be faithful to guide her continually. Her life led her to choose God or to choose the gods of her homeland. Our lives do the same.

The place we choose to go and lodge today is more a matter of heart than real estate. Ruth needed to go to a physical place to complete her work for the Lord. Maybe you do, too, and if that's the case, He will show you the opportunity to go there. And if not, He will give you the wisdom to see how to work in the place in which you dwell now.

Either way, when you choose to live with all the conviction of Ruth, God blesses you with a *treasure of place* that reminds you that your place is right beside Him, because He's still here. Ruth knew her physical place because she knew her spiritual place—in God's heart. We can have that same wisdom and faith when we make the choice for God and forsake any false gods that would claim us today, gods of greed or envy or anything else in this physical world.

We find our place when we fill everything up with the Lord, a place of peace and purpose that we know well because we know *Who He is.* Ruth went from a poor widow to the great-grandmother of David, all because she knew her place. The treasures of abundance will overflow for us, too, when we know ours. We can go any physical place because our spiritual place never moves.

> *Now thanks be to God who always leads us in triumph in Christ, and through us diffuses the fragrance of His knowledge in every place.*
>
> 2 CORINTHIANS 2:14 NKJV

Treasures of Circumstance

Jesus knew the work was hard, but He called seventy followers to go out before Him anyway. "Go your way; behold, I send you out as lambs among wolves" (Luke 10:3 NKJV).

Were they afraid? Were they excited? I don't know, but they were faithful and obedient, trusting what their Lord told them. No matter what they might encounter or what evils might await them, they were secure because they carried the peace of Jesus with them, and they could not lose it (verse 6). We are called to do the same.

We may not find ourselves face-to-face with those who are sick or those who don't believe every day, but we do face circumstances that threaten our peace every day. With what appears to be little instruction, Jesus entrusted those seventy with His message. The message is the same for us to deliver now, and through every circumstance, we grow wiser and more able to do as we're called.

And when things go badly for us, when we feel overwhelmed with the world and less than able to go on, we are reminded that as long as we do what we know how to do, we will not go wrong.

> *Then the seventy returned with joy, saying, "Lord, even the demons are subject to us in Your name."*
>
> LUKE 10:17 NKJV

The faith of the seventy made them wise, and their trust made them secure. What "demons" are you running into today? What situations are you facing that call for your wisdom and faith? Where are you going now, and are you carrying the peace of Jesus with you?

Prepare for your journey, and watch God bless you with a *treasure of circumstance* by filling your heart with the wisdom to harvest from the great bounty, wherever He leads you. Every day, every moment is like a city that the seventy visited— unknown at first but housing a victory meant just for you. Don't miss these treasures of God's faithfulness. Go, look, draw on what you've learned to guide you through anything; the treasure of the Lord's security will hold you tightly along the way.

Know that nothing is by accident and nothing is fruitless. Every circumstance is a treasure waiting to happen.

> *"For I will give you words and wisdom that none of your adversaries will be able to resist or contradict."*
>
> LUKE 21:15 NIV

✳ ✳ ✳

"Well, I reckon You were right, Lord."

"Most likely."

"I mean, *look* how You're right: There is no project, place, or circumstance where You won't be. There is no end to Your faithfulness in everything in my life, and I'll never step outside Your wisdom, no matter where I go."

"I told you, like an unlimited account."

"The day's not over yet—maybe You'd like to rethink that promise. This is *me*, remember?"

"Irrelevant, even in your case. This is *Me*, remember?"

Oh, yeah. I knew that.

For no matter how many promises God has made, they are "Yes" in Christ.

2 CORINTHIANS 1:20 NIV

Chapter 33

Just Passing Through

"When you pass through the waters, I will be with you; and through the rivers, they shall not overflow you. When you walk through the fire, you shall not be burned, nor shall the flame scorch you. For I am the LORD your God."

ISAIAH 43:2–3 NKJV

Sometimes our lives can feel like nothing but overflowing waters and scorching flames, can't they? That's when even the tunnel is nowhere to be seen, let alone the light. The insecurity is alive and kicking, and it's during those less-than-wonderful times that we have to remember all we've learned. It's like a ticket to a better destination.

If we call on our knowledge of the Lord during those times, we can go step-by-step through the pain as we cling to every faithful trait. The waters aren't so strong when we call on God's strength to hold us up. The flames aren't so powerful when we trust in God's power to help us overcome. Nothing we'll ever encounter here is wiser than the Lord, and our job is to trust His control and command of everything we see and everything we don't.

* * *

"Lord, sometimes I think there are tough times that will never end. Where are You then?"

"I'm right where I've always been, at your side, waiting on your call."

"How can I survive these times that hurt so much?"

"Hold on to Me. We're just passing through."

"To where? I can't see beyond the pain."

"To where you're called, My child. These tough times are interruptions, nothing more. Nothing can stop you when I've told you to go. I know the way."

"But what about me? Will I know the way?"

"Of course, when you know Me."

"How'd I know we'd come back to this? Is that the beginning of everything?"

"That *is* everything."

* * *

What comfort! What delight! The Lord had simplified yet another insecurity. Everything that hurts is neither unstoppable flood nor unquench-able flame; it's just another part of my life. Knowing God keeps the disasters in perspective. Knowing that He's not abandoned His plan for me makes passing through the messes another chance to learn.

How can I be afraid or lonely or confused if the Lord knows where I'm going? How can I worry that an interruption to His plan is bigger than He is? How can I lose my faith in the God who lives in my soul and knows everything I need before I do? How can I forget what He's taught me so patiently and completely? How can I doubt that He'll lead me through every hurt and remain faithful to His promise to be with me?

I can't because He's right: I can't do any of those things if I know *Who He is.*

> *For this God is our God for ever and ever;*
> *he will be our guide even to the end.*

> PSALM 48:14 NIV

 Chapter 34

Going For a Walk

The Lord tells me not to be afraid of the storms of my life, to trust in His wisdom even when I don't know where to go next. He says I can still keep going if I know Who I'm going with. Never misses a chance to make His point, does He?

> *If we live in the Spirit, let us also walk in the Spirit.*
>
> GALATIANS 5:25 NKJV

The "going" follows the "knowing." If we *know* the Lord and delight in His faithfulness, we can *go* everywhere with the security that only comes from Him. If we don't know Him, we are stuck, mired in the ugliest pit of insecurity we've ever seen. It's like having the navigational sense of a hammer. We, too, are worthless on our own and desperately in need of direction and control.

And wise far beyond our embarrassingly feeble

means, the Lord spells things out pretty simply for us. *"Know Me and let's go,"* He says. Every day is another chance to be His child, a chance to see where He leads, a chance to leave the insecurity a little further behind.

He invites us to walk *with* Him, not at a distance where we can't touch Him, not ahead where we must go afraid, and not at a pace other than the one that we need. Every step is a journey under His perfect orchestration.

> *And what does the LORD require of you*
> *but to do justly, to love mercy, and to walk*
> *humbly with your God?*
>
> MICAH 6:8 NKJV

Walking Humbly

This command becomes easier and easier the better we know our God. When we don't know Him well, it's hard to turn ourselves over to Him in complete assurance that He will do what He says. But the more we know, the more this command becomes a blessing than a requirement. What else *would* we do?

Our walk with the Lord is our every breath with the Lord. Every entreaty is made in faith, every question asked in confidence. Our humility is our trust that He is great enough and faithful enough to be the God He claims to be. And we learn that we are the loved and cherished children He says we are.

Because He is just and merciful, He comes to dwell in me, His Spirit intertwined in mine. Because He is just and merciful *and* faithful to teach me the same, I can dwell in Him; and together we will go wherever He needs me to go. It is a walk that never ends, a security that never fails because of *Who He is.*

*God, who has called you into fellowship
with his Son Jesus Christ our Lord, is
faithful.*

1 CORINTHIANS 1:9 NIV

Chapter 35

You Are Still Here, Lord!

"The LORD himself goes before you and will be with you; he will never leave you nor forsake you. Do not be afraid; do not be discouraged."

DEUTERONOMY 31:8 NIV

"You were right—of course. This has been a wild ride, Lord!"

"Told you. And it will only get better."

"I believe You! There is so much I want to do, and I don't feel insecure anymore."

"Good. When you know *Who I am,* you know who you are, and you know where you can go. There is nothing to fear."

And still so much to learn. . .

There's Nowhere He Isn't

Learning to know God is learning to know thought and air and being—because there is no place He doesn't live. There is no place He can't reach us and no place He won't heal us. He is as close as we allow Him to be and more faithful than the sunrise. He teaches us everything we need to know, and then He goes with us everywhere we need to go. We can't hide, but guess what? Neither can He.

His character is unchangeable, and His power is unmatched. He knows all of our failings and faults, but He never goes away. His wisdom allows Him to see beyond the temporary worries that strangle us, and His love for us sits Him beside us while we recover. He never lets go, and our learning continues.

> *For great is his love toward us, and the*
> *faithfulness of the LORD endures forever.*
> *Praise the LORD.*
>
> PSALM 117:2 NIV

✳   ✳   ✳

"You're very brave, Lord. I know it hasn't been easy walking with me through my life, especially when we started this journey and I knew so little."

"But look at what you know now!"

"I know You, and I know that You *are* still here, Lord!"

"Are you surprised?"

"Not anymore, because I know that my security is one of Your specialties."

"You're right, and I will be here with you still and always. Will *you* be here with *Me,* still and always?"

"Without a doubt! Being here with You is my *only* specialty."

"What a plan—it's the only one you need."

"I have called you by your name; you are Mine."

ISAIAH 43:1 NKJV

✱ ✱ ✱

God's faithfulness is God's wisdom. *He says to me, "There is wisdom for everything you need to do living in your heart, where I am. Every moment of your life is a moment with Me, and every step you take is a step with Me when you trust in My devotion to you and My complete control of everything you are. I have you right where I want you, and from here we can go anywhere because I know the way.* ***That wisdom is Who I am.****"*

To Know, To Go—in God's Wisdom

- How can you know in the dark? How will you rest in God's wisdom when you can't see your own? What does it mean to know that God is a part of you and that you are a part of Him?
- What does believing have to do with knowing? Why can't you *go* until you *know* and *believe* God's faithfulness?
- What do you know about yourself because you know God? How does He always know what you need to take your next step? How will you love Him back today?
- What treasures are you storing in your heart? How will you use this banked knowledge, as opportunities of *project, place,* and *circumstance* arrive?
- What tough times are you passing through right now? Do you believe that the Lord's wisdom is enough to guide you through them and beyond? How does knowing *Who He is* change your perception of those tough times?
- How is your walk with the Lord? Are you staying close to Him and drawing on His wisdom for every step you take? What happens to your insecurity when you walk with Him?

- Have you ever found yourself anywhere that God wasn't? How will the knowledge that He is *still here* with you change the rest of your life?

* * *

Lord, in Your wisdom, I find Your infallible care and concern for me, and I'm amazed. In every tiny fleck of the breath that gives me life, You live. I cannot be outside the reach of Your knowledge of me. Because You're here, still and always, I can draw on Your wisdom in every project, place, and circumstance of my life. I can go and work, rest, and then go again; and through it all I will know more about **Who You are** *and be secure as I walk in the wisdom of Your faithfulness. Thank You for loving me. Amen.*

Contact the Author:

Karon Goodman
P. O. Box 3226
Oxford, Alabama 36203

If you enjoyed

You Still Here, Lord?

be sure to read these other titles by
KARON PHILLIPS GOODMAN

You're Late Again, Lord!
*The Impatient Woman's Guide
to God's Timing*
ISBN 1-58660-410-4
Witty writing and thoughtful insights
for any woman who's questioned God's
timing, with encouragement to spend
your waiting time purposefully.

Grab a Broom, Lord—
There's Dust Everywhere!
*The Imperfect Woman's Guide
to God's Grace*
ISBN 1-58660-918-1
God's grace is more powerful than life's
imperfections, as you'll discover in this
delightfully wise guide to living a full,
powerful life in the security of God's grace.

ONLY $4.97 EACH!

Available wherever Christian books are sold.
Or order from:

Barbour Publishing, Inc.
P.O. Box 719
Uhrichsville, Ohio 44683
www.barbourbooks.com

If you order by mail, add $2.00 to your order for shipping.
Prices are subject to change without notice.